THE GIFT OF EXPERIENCE

Remarkable Encounters and Misadventures

in the Global Pursuit of Waves

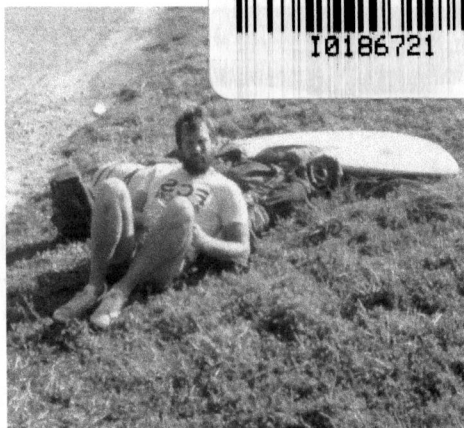

HARVEY ZENDT

DEDICATION

I would like to dedicate this book to the memory of two special people who made me a better traveler and person through their joie de vivre and spirit of adventure.

My father spoke infrequently of his trip around the world but shared just enough to really inspire me. I remember him saying that one can- not truly understand the human spirit without going to India and engaging with the fascinating people there. He also talked of his time in the South Pacific as special for many reasons, in particular how living on an island in the middle of a vast ocean with little contact with the outside world was a blessing in many ways—wholesome simplicity and living close to nature without many of the trappings of modern society. I do not regret having followed his suggestions.

I first met Tom Robinson on the soccer field, my freshman year in col- lege. We quickly discovered our shared passion for surfing, and I was impressed with his stories of growing up in Hawaii, the mecca of the sport. We spent spring vacations together, we surfed in Florida, we hitchhiked across the country to surf in California one summer, and we spent a magical winter living out of a car in Hawaii. We even taught together for a few years at a school outside of

Philadelphia. In all of those experiences, Tom's sense of humor, intel- ligence, morality, and grit made him a joy to be with. I am a better person for the time I spent with him.

"I didn't learn until I was in college about other cultures, and I should have learned that in the first grade. A first grader should understand that his or her culture isn't a rational invention; that there are thousands of other cultures and they all work pretty well; that all cultures function on faith rather than truth; that there are lots of alternatives to our own society. Cultural relativity is defensible and attractive. It's also a source of hope. It means we don't have to continue this way if we don't like it."

KURT VONNEGUT

═══════════

COVER PHOTOGRAPHS:

George Zendt, author's father, in front of the Taj Mahal, Agra, India, 1935

Harvey Zendt, author, by the side of the road, Garden Route, South Africa, 1983

CONTENTS

Introduction   ix

1. The Lost Art of the Thumb   1
2. A Special Place, Rincon, Puerto Rico | 1969, 1971   11
3. My Itinerary | 1976, 1977   21
4. Danger and Misadventures, Costa Rica | 1976   28
5. Crossing Borders, Guatemala and Mexico | 1976   36
6. Localism: Hawaii, Western Samoa, Costa Rica, Nepal,
   El Salvador | 1976-77   43
7. Hawaiian Winter | 1976-77   55
8. Cooking with the Krishnas, Australia | 1977   64
9. Finding Uluwatu and a Coke, Indonesia | 1977   72
10. Beyond Explanation, Malaysia | 1977   82
11. A Burmese Marriage, Myanmar | 1977   92
12. The Goodness of People, Sri Lanka, India, Poland | 1977   102
13. Encountering Apartheid, South Africa | 1983   114
14. My Father's Story, Asia and the South Pacific | 1935   128
15. Recognition and Appreciation   134

INTRODUCTION

────────────

THE SPOT WAS PERFECT, RIGHT ON THE POINT AT SUN-zal, just a few yards from the excellent break, no noise except for the sounds of the ocean, a bit of shade from the nearby coconut trees, and remote, but not too far from the main road. We had come here to escape the hustle and bustle of La Libertad and have some excellent waves all to ourselves.

The two-story home itself was quite rustic, made entirely out of bamboo with the exception of the brick cooking area, which had no walls but a ceiling held up by wooden posts, which was also the floor of the second story. You climbed a rickety wooden ladder to get upstairs, which included nothing more than a room with a loft above it. There was a crude outhouse about ten yards away and fresh water at a nearby pump.

We were told that a surfer from California had designed and built the unique structure, but was rarely there. The only neighbors, a family of five, looked after it.

When we asked about the rent, Leda, the mother, informed us that it was ten dollars a month. We did not hesitate to say we would like to stay there for a few weeks. Minutes later, her husband arrived to inform us that his wife had misspoken. Here came reality; we expected the worst. He said it was actually thirteen dollars a month. We were in.

Living there was a small step above camping out, cooking on an open fire, sleeping on a wooden floor, climbing the precarious ladder to go to bed, and descending it for a midnight pee. The dwelling had no electricity or refrigeration, and procuring food necessitated a ten-minute hike on a dirt path, followed by a long walk on the main road. We ended up staying for two months, surfing its great waves every day, connecting with some fascinating locals as well as adventurous travelers from a number of countries, and creating a sense of home in this rustic abode.

Today, you can go on the internet and book a room in Sunzal for $40 to $340 per night. There are surf camps, restaurants, and nightlife up the beach. The waves are still excellent, but our experience there in 1976 cannot be duplicated.

I am sharing my experiences, such as this one, because certain aspects of the world as we knew it in the 1970s have evolved dramatically or no longer exist. I was inspired to write these stories after reading the diary of my father, who went around the world in 1935. Like me, he had experienced a life that had changed significantly. His stories of big game hunting in what was French Indochina and being stranded on a South Pacific Island for two months without any money or belongings, because the mail boat on which he was traveling left port early, inspired me to leave my teaching job in Philadelphia in 1976 and explore foreign lands. I had become a passionate surfer and wanted to ride the best waves in the world, but my goal was also to connect with cultures that were different from mine in suburban America of the 1970s.

My stories focus mostly on an eighteen-month round-the-world trip in 1976-77, but also include experiences from other adventures. I have written these narratives based on my recollection, notes from a diary, and collaboration with some of my friends whom I met along the way. The accounts are as accurate as memory allows. I have a little sense of nostalgia in sharing them, knowing that many could not be relived in 2025. I recognize that there are different kinds of exciting adventures today that did not exist then, reaching new spots on our planet or going into outer space, for example. Do these new opportunities provide the chances for transformative moments like the ones from which I benefited? Is the world better or worse for what is no more and what is new? I do not try to answer those questions in this book. I simply want to share my experiences to give the reader some insights into what life was like from my perspective back then and the ways it was life-changing for me.

Finally, I want to note that while the people, the various cultures, and the wonders of nature provided the basis for most of my experiences, there were sociopolitical elements in the countries I visited that accentuated what I encountered. Here are a few examples:

Being an American in Southeast Asia in the 1970s made it virtually impossible to avoid the impact of the Vietnam War. On my first evening on the Thai Island of Ko Samui, I dined with the District Governor and was enlightened by his perspective on the war. According to him, after World War II, Southeast Asian countries had a choice to side with the United States or China. Thailand, like most nations, chose the U.S. because they felt secure that we would support them as needed.

When our nation gave up on Vietnam, that trust was diminished significantly. Naturally, I explained the rationale for my support for the withdrawal, but never forgot his persuasive perspective regarding our country's actions.

During my time in India, Prime Minister Indira Gandhi had just begun her attempt at forced sterilization of women as a way to deal with the exploding population. While this extremely controversial program was short-lived, over eleven million women were impacted, and the country was in a minor state of turmoil as a result. The topic surfaced frequently in conversations, and I had to be careful how to share my opinion, wanting to be true to my convictions without offending others.

Throughout my travels, I intuitively knew I needed to be sensitive to the issues facing the countries I visited: the treatment of the Indigenous People in Australia, the civil war in El Salvador, apartheid in South Africa, and the tension with the Tibetans in Nepal, to name a few. As I traveled, I learned how to navigate my engagement with locals regarding sensitive topics, without significantly compromising my beliefs, but I know mistakes were made. Yet my personal exposure to these realities provided an enhanced understanding of the diversity and complexity of the human experience.

I have the deepest gratitude to my father for his example and inspiration to travel the world. While he did not talk often of his experiences, they would surface periodically in various conversations, demonstrating insights and perspectives that he had garnered from his trip. Most importantly, my confidence to step out of my comfort zone to travel as I did came in large part from knowing his story, and an awareness that it was much more challenging in 1935, as world knowledge and ease of travel were significantly less in his time. I thought it important to share a few of his stories in this collection of my travel experiences as a point of reference and a tribute to him.

AUTHOR'S NOTES

Sunzal is a rural community a few miles north of the port of La Libertad in El Salvador. In the 1970s, the country was still a very violent one due to its dense population and lengthy civil war that was caused by a repressive military government and significant inequality in life amongst its people. Although we had to be careful with our belongings (and ourselves), we traveled there because it has the most consistent surf in Latin America. La Libertad has a world-class point break, and in the '70s, a small population of itinerant surfers made it home. There was a restaurant right on the point run by a famous

Long Island surfer, a great place for a meal and gathering insights regarding the surf and local culture.

While we enjoyed La Libertad for many reasons, we wanted to settle where there was good surf without the crowds and other urban issues, so on a tip from a local, we took the bus a few miles up the coast to the village of Sunzal and moved into the cottage right on the point.

There were many magical moments in our time there, often surfing with the gigantic manta rays, many of which had a fin span of over twenty feet, whose tips looked hauntingly like giant shark fins, a source of unease until we got used to them. Our neighbors treated us like family, and playing with their children brought almost as much joy as riding the great waves. Of all the living arrangements in my global travels, Sunzal was one of the best.

Our landlords

The crew in front of the hut in Sunzal

THE LOST ART OF THE THUMB

═══════

I TURNED TO SEE HOW MY BUDDY WAS DOING IN THE cramped back seat. Observing his attempt to wake up, I couldn't help but laugh.

"What are you grinning at?" asked Tom confusedly as he eased from sleep into consciousness. "Looks like we're just passing Chicago! Should we get out at the next exit?"

"Nope! This ride is going all the way to New York City!"

It had been quite a few days since we had left the comfort of friends in the Bay Area and embarked on a marathon hitchhiking excursion across the country. In a little over forty-eight hours, we had the good fortune of finding lengthy rides with a variety of drivers in record time. Near the Iowa / Illinois border, we had been picked up by a farm boy who was out for the adventure of his life, which for him meant the big city of Chicago. Within the first thirty minutes, I had convinced our friendly Iowan driver that if he really wanted to see the big city, he should go to New York rather than Chicago. My enthusiastic pitch generated some sincere excitement on his part, and the temptation of seeing sites such as Times Square, the Statue of Liberty, and Yankee Stadium outweighed his financial and time concerns of extending the trip.

This change of plans eliminated our worry about navigating the next span of 1000 miles and allowed us to have bragging rights of crossing the continent in three days. However, we did have to keep our Iowa friend entertained and content with his decision, particularly when we were stuck in traffic numerous times around some large cities in Ohio and Pennsylvania.

Our strategy on this cross-country trip had been for Tom, the more presentable of the duo, to be the active "thumber" on the side of the road while I rested, and once in the car, Tom would nap in the back seat while I chatted with the driver, hoping to convince him or her that picking us up was a good decision.

Why do we no longer see people by the side of the road with their thumbs out or displaying a sign noting their destination? During our trip across the country and up and down the California coast in 1970, there were times when we arrived at an exit on the Pacific Coast Highway and disappointingly saw a long line of over thirty fellow "thumbers" ahead of us. Our choice at that point was to go to the end of the line and wait patiently for our turn, or start walking up the highway away from the masses to escape the competition and hopefully procure a ride more quickly. The latter choice was against the hitchhikers' code of proper behavior and, on certain stretches of road, unsafe, but sometimes we would risk it. Today, the sight of a long line for travelers only exists at a taxi stand, as the practice of hitchhiking seems to be almost nonexistent.

There are good reasons for this mode of transportation: it's the cheapest way to travel; it is keeping at least one more car off the road to diminish pollution and congestion in a minuscule way; it offers adventure and an opportunity to engage with a myriad of people (even if they are not of your choosing), and you can gain insights into places and ways of life about which previously you knew little or nothing. Of course, there are obvious negatives—you can't be in a rush; there are dangers, and you need to be ready to be uncomfortable, tired, and hungry for extended periods of time.

While Tom and I relished the experience of that summer, there were numerous hair-raising moments. Once, as we were heading into San Diego, our driver did not want to arrive home in the middle of the night, so we pulled into a rest stop in the mountains just east of the city. It was not easy for three of us to sleep in the tiny Rambler sedan, but somehow I was blessed with the entire back seat. This was wonderful, until I was roused from my deep slumber by a loud, threatening truck driver waving a pistol at Tom, bellowing, "You tried to roll that guy! It's guys like you that make places like this unsafe." Tom immediately turned on his most polite, eloquent demeanor to diffuse the situation and calm down all those involved in the altercation.

To understand the circumstances, it helps to know the backstory. While traveling earlier in the trip, I had once jumped into an abandoned car for a resting spot. This night, Tom had just visited the men's room and, upon returning, saw someone asleep in a nearby car. For some reason, he assumed it was once again me choosing an alternative resting place and began to shake the body to get up, but it wasn't me! It was a boy whose mother was returning to the car and, upon seeing Tom rousting her son, began to scream. The noise brought on the gun-toting truck driver. Suffice it to say, we charmed our way out of the predicament and made a quick exit from the rest stop with no way to go back to sleep and a lasting memory.

There were many other "life-stretching" experiences in our travels that tested our ability to connect and not offend the diverse group of people who were kind enough to offer us a ride. Of course, convincing someone that our surfboard could fit into an already crowded car, when there was barely room for us, was an ongoing challenge.

Tom and I turned down a ride late at night just outside of Laramie, Wyoming, from a bunch of cowboys in a pickup truck after we had already been escorted out of town by the police, who did not want hitchhikers within the city limits. We were weary and had been standing for a while by the edge of this dark, empty stretch of road, anxious to keep moving east. The truck had initially passed us heading into town with a bunch of hoots coming from its rowdy occupants. Then it turned around and stopped in front of us with the devilish smiling passenger in the front seat bellowing, "We'd be glad to show you boys the Wyoming countryside."

Despite our desire for a ride, we sensed serious trouble, and Tom quickly replied, "Thanks, but we think we will stay put for the evening." Fortunately, the cowboys did not want to convince us further and sped off, leaving us covered in dust, the only negative consequence of the nerve-racking encounter. Shortly thereafter, and to our relief, a more wholesome driver picked us up.

The most memorable exchange on the trip was my attempt at a rational conversation with a disheveled free spirit, who picked us up around Big Sur in California and was promoting "cannibalism" as a partial solution to the world's food shortage. His theory was that uncontaminated dead bodies are a viable food source being ignored by our leaders. He claimed that he had nibbled on a finger of a deceased friend once, and it tasted fine. My reactions combined fear (Is the driver planning to harm us? This was the summer of Charles Manson!) along with the tension of trying to engage in a serious conversation without disclosing my honest feeling that our driver had done a few too many drugs, which had led to such crazy life perspectives.

I couldn't help but think of Jonathon Swift's famous essay, "A Modest Proposal," which recommended the Irish give up their children for food during the famous famine, but I did not refer to it, as I feared encouraging the bizarre sentiment of the driver. Fortunately, the ride was short, and we exited the van safely with my last comment being, "Enjoyed the conversation and thanks for the lift," as I rolled my eyes and smiled at Tom.

On this cross-country trip, Tom and I parted ways in the middle of the night at a rest stop on the Pennsylvania Turnpike. Tom was continuing on to New York City with our newfound Midwestern friend, while I would search for one last ride to Philadelphia. After three days on the road, we were a bit disheveled physically and mentally, and I was not looking forward to finding a ride for this last portion by myself, especially at this hour of the night. Fortunately, I noticed a Volkswagen in the parking lot of the rest stop with a dealer plate from Jenkintown, which was near where I lived. When two girls emerged from the restaurant and headed towards the Volkswagen, I garnered what charm I had left and asked them if they were going to Jenkintown, and if so, could they give me a ride. There was an understandable hesitation in their response, so I asked them if they knew a friend of mine who lived there. Incredibly, they did, and within minutes, I was in the back seat, headed home.

Most of our rides that summer landed somewhere between fascinating and uneventful. Some led to places to stay and a good meal; others resulted in an exit at a slightly undesirable spot, which required our resourcefulness to continue. No doubt the experience allowed us to grow in unexpected ways and bundle up some great memories. Most importantly, it convinced me that opportunities to hitchhike should be a part of my life going forward.

As I hitched more, I learned valuable lessons—always look into the eyes of the driver, be as kempt as possible; if you are carrying a surfboard, size up when it is best to display it and when it is best to hide it from view, the same goes for hitching with other people. But always have the most attractive member of the group, usually not me, on display.

Seven years later, in 1977, I embarked on a round-the-world surf trip. In those two years of international exploration, I used every imaginable form of transportation, but it was hitchhiking that played the most important role in my travels and enhanced my experience tremendously. Some countries were easier to find rides in than others, with New Zealand being the best. People there were so willing to help, as exemplified by an Auckland city bus stopping and giving me a ride to my destination, even though I was just walking down the road and home was off his route. All this help at no charge. I was amazed at the generosity of the driver as well as the patience of the passengers who accepted a longer ride just to help out this visiting surfer.

Hitchhiking throughout New Zealand led to contact with a myriad of colorful characters, lots of good meals, places to stay, and an enhanced appreciation for the goodness of humanity. My group by the side of the road varied from two couples to just me, and rides were abundant in all cases. One driver was the owner of a large camp, who not only gave us a long ride but invited us to stay for a few days at his home, where we rode horses, water skied, and delighted in thrilling rides on a cart running down an old train rail to a pristine lake. Another fellow drove us a long distance and then convinced us to stay at the campground he was managing, wanting us to run the business at night for him, so he could enjoy the local nightlife.

To be truthful, there was one blemish regarding my observations of the wholesome Kiwis. Two girls, whom we did not know, were arrested for a hitching scam. After being picked up, they would threaten to accuse the driver of attempted sexual assault unless he took them where they wanted to go and gave them some money or food. Fortunately, a few of the victims reported them to the local police, and they were subsequently apprehended.

Hitchhiking in Australia provided similar experiences to those in New Zealand. The highlight was traveling with the crew that operated the largest Ferris Wheel in the country. While the seating was a bit cramped in the cab of their huge trailer, it was a great way to see the countryside and a fascinating opportunity to learn about this unique facet of Aussie life. The crew shared a multitude of hilarious, hair-raising tales of miscues setting up and operating the wheel, and we attracted quite the attention from locals at every gas and food stop.

Years later, in 1983, my wife and I enjoyed a three-month honeymoon in South Africa that involved a fair bit of hitchhiking. The country was still in the grips of apartheid, which resulted in some awkward situations, as we vehemently opposed the country's practice but wanted to be courteous to the many kind and generous people we encountered and hoped to better understand. This was a constant challenge in an otherwise wonderful experience. We found South Africans very generous, offering us rides and memorable forms of hospitality. The most remarkable encounter began on the road from Port Elizabeth to Cape Town, along the Garden Route. Cedric, a traveling salesman, picked us up, and we hit it off so well that we stayed in his company for three days. He would take us to a town, drop us off at the beach, make his calls, and then retrieve us later to head off to the next stop. At the last town each day, we would have dinner together, he would leave us at the campground, go on to his hotel, and then take off again with us honeymooners the next morning. He seemed to love the adventure as much as we did.

We parted ways as we neared Cape Town, but that was not the end of our time with Cedric. A few weeks later, when we retraced our route north on the same highway, a car stopped to pick us up, and when we engaged with the driver, his first words were, "You must be Harvey and Louisa!" It was Cedric's *brother*—he had been told to keep an eye out for an American couple with a surfboard by the side of the road. He happily delivered us to Cedric's house, where we spent a delightful few days with his large, extended family.

Life in the States has evolved, in some ways, for the better, but this roadside activity is rarely seen today. Do people feel less safe, less trusting, or is it just a matter of some ways of life simply running their course?

How lucky was I that I grew up in a time when the hitchhiking experience was possible? I will hold onto the excitement I always felt when waiting by the side of the road, thumb out, with cars whizzing by. I would turn to see a car on the shoulder, quickly run to the side door, and with my eager smile, utter a thanks and the query, "Where are you headed?"

AUTHOR'S NOTES

The practice of hitchhiking began in the United States in the early 1900s and spread to Europe shortly thereafter. Its evolution grew with the popularity and style of the automobile and the roads on which they travelled.

It should be noted that the success of hitchhiking is dependent a great deal on location. There are some areas where the practice is frowned upon or even against the law. Police in six states where it is illegal will actually give you a ticket or worse if you are hitchhiking in their vicinity. For example, a foreign couple was recently fined $525 in Arizona. These regulations have been enforced primarily for safety reasons.

On the other hand, some countries encourage the practice. Government vehicles in Cuba are required to pick up hitchhikers, as there is a car shortage, and up until the 1990s, the government of Poland distributed coupons that hitchhikers gave to drivers when they received a ride, and prizes were given to those citizens with the highest number of them at the end of each year. Germany and Austria have recently taken various steps to make the practice easier, as they feel it is good for the environment (fewer cars on the road) and provides opportunities for healthy social interaction.

My experience hitchhiking in South Africa was unique, as it was during the apartheid years, and it was understood that whites did not try to get rides from others. The drivers who picked us up always assumed we were foreign travelers, and we saw very few other hitchhikers by the side of the road.

Exit from a California ride

On the road in New Zealand with Bob and Barb

Riding with the crew from the largest Ferris wheel in Australia

*The start of our three-day hitch across the US in front of
the house boat/caboose of a friend in Sausalito*

A SPECIAL PLACE, RINCON,
PUERTO RICO | 1969, 1971

OVER THE COURSE OF THREE DECADES, I BECAME MUCH wiser about entering unfamiliar places around the world. As a nineteen-year-old, off on my first adventure, I traveled alone to Rincon, Puerto Rico, quite clueless about things to consider. Before this trip, I had never traveled without my buds nor beyond the East Coast of the United States, nor to a place with large, powerful surf, breaking over coral reefs. Although I gained important experience and knowledge between my first trip to Rincon and my second, I made rookie mistakes in both.

I had read about this amazing place in Surfer Magazine the year before, in 1968, when this town of 9,000 people hosted the World Surfing Championships. I was enticed by Rincon's beautiful waves and stories. Through the magazine article, I learned that I could contact someone named Kahuna, a person who allegedly helped visiting surfers. With no other viable options, I reached out to him, and he agreed to meet me upon my arrival in Puerto Rico.

Sure enough, to my relief, when I got off the plane, I could see a smiling face with a sign "Kahuna" amid the sweltering crowd at the San Juan airport. Kahuna was incredibly welcoming, and he engaged me with stories the entire ride to Rincon, which greatly lessened my trepidation regarding what lay ahead, but not entirely. The trip had already been a life-stretching experience, landing in a mostly non-English speaking airport alone with only a rough idea of my destination and no plans to connect with anyone when I arrived at the beach town.

For starters, I thought Rincon was an hour from the airport. It was three hours away, which meant Kahuna dropped me off at my planned destination around sunset. I had counted on just sleeping on the beach the first night, but had not considered the higher tide, due to the large swell, leaving only a small dry portion with little sand to set up a precarious campsite. Consequently, I needed to go to plan B for sleeping, whatever that was.

With no clear alternative, I began to walk back up the dirt road, which was surrounded by sugar cane fields, another poor option for a night's rest, as there was not much open space and they were known to be homes for snakes, creatures which were not welcome in my sleeping bag! Although the sun was setting, it was still quite hot. I was beginning to feel the weight of my backpack and board, and wondering what I would do if I did not find a place to stay. Fatigue and worry churned in my stomach. I began to doubt my ability to handle this experience, and it was only the first day, when suddenly I heard Jimi Hendrix's "Purple Haze" coming from a small wooden home at the end of a dusty driveway.

Out of options, I followed the music, hoping to find a place to stay for the night. As I approached the rickety structure, barely larger than a mobile home, I could see the front was raised up on cinder blocks and posts, and the music was coming from a small room beneath the porch. Putting down my gear, I gently opened the door to a frenetic scene of three surfers sanding a board amid a notice-able layer of cannabis smoke. Without missing a beat, one of them handed me a block and said to work on the front left portion.

The intense process went on for a few more minutes until everyone paused, and one fellow asked, "Who are you?" I sheep-ishly explained my situation, and in response, another guy grunted without much positivity that I could spend the night. The next few hours were an unsettled blur with one notably embarrassing moment. The combination of the heat, my nerves from the whole experience, lack of food, and the secondhand strong marijuana smoke took a toll on my system.

The awkward encounter began with me sitting on the hood of their rusty "clunker" truck, listening to the most outspoken of the crew explaining their story. They were Hawaiians who were fed up with the crowds at home and were starting over in Rincon, as it had great waves without the many complexities of Hawaii, and the cost of living was much more manageable for a surfer's meager income. As the conversation turned to the large waves in Rincon, my stomach became uneasy. I could feel a bit of vomit rise up through my throat, and as it emerged, I subtly collected it in my hand and nonchalantly wiped it behind me on the rusted hood. Fortunately, the storyteller was so absorbed with his tale that he did not notice.

I was saved from this embarrassing moment by the one woman in the crew, calling out that dinner was ready. Relieved that I was included, the healthy spread settled my stomach, and I began to feel some level of comfort with this group of Hawaiian surfers, knowing I had a safe place to sleep. After dinner, they introduced me to the recently released Rolling Stones album, "Let It Bleed," followed by fascinating surf talk, though my contributions to the chat were infantile compared to the more veteran members of the household. As the evening was winding down, I felt an overwhelming sense of relief. I had made it through the gauntlet of fire, found food, a place to rest, and people who would help me find decent lodging. To this day, the Stones' "You Can't Always Get What You Want" remains one of my all-time favorite songs, as it is a reminder of one of the more memorable evenings of my youth.

When the crew headed for bed, I was relegated to the porch for sleeping and rested relatively well until the roosters began their morning reveille, followed by someone peeing out the window right near my head. After a quick breakfast, the crew piled into the truck to head for the waves. They told me to bring all my gear, and they would leave me at a spot where I could find a place to stay.

The swell had not dropped a bit overnight, and I tried desperately to prove myself with these characters in some very intimidating surf. Being from Hawaii, they were right at home in the powerful waves and rode them playfully. On the other hand, this Jersey surfer was on edge most of the time, my worries vacillating between getting a good ride to earn acceptance and not sustaining any injuries. Surfing large waves over a jagged coral reef is a drastically different experience from riding easy, smaller ones over forgiving sand bars at my home break. Hitting the bottom in New Jersey might result in a sore neck; here, it could get you a serious gash, which might require stitches or something even worse! Though rare, a few surfers die each year from surfing big waves over coral, something that was on my mind that first morning.

After a memorable surf session with my new friends, I splurged on a $10/night bungalow and slowly started to up my comfort level both on land and in the water. Within a few days, the experience that had initially been so intimidating was now pure enjoyment, for the most part. By the time I had to head home, I had no regrets. Rincon was special. I had overcome my jitters of solo travel and big waves the first few days and knew this was a place to which I would visit again.

Back home, I shared my enthusiasm for Rincon with a number of fellow surfers and a year later returned with four friends. This time, I was not a newcomer but a veteran who still made some rookie mistakes. On my first trip, I had scoped out a good spot to sleep on the beach, and this is where my four buddies and I set up camp. It was a wide stretch of pure sand, thirty feet from the edge of the water, with quasi-jungle and sugar cane fields just inland. There were other characters in our beach camp "neighborhood" that added to the social dynamic. One fellow named Sharky had carved his own cutlery from some local hardwood, refusing to let anything metal touch his lips. He had set up his home in the trees! There was also a non-surfing group of eccentric characters from New England staying at this spot, who were there more for the tropical beach scene than the waves.

In between great surf sessions, we had fascinating experiences on land. We engaged with Dogman, an elderly local who meandered up and down the beach with his pack of dogs and a bag of coconuts. He gave us insights into the history and physical attributes of some of the local beaches, including Domes, Sandy Beach, and Steps. He was very accepting of the surfers who came to his town, enjoying watching them in the water, and in turn, the surfers named one of the best breaks in Rincon after him. It's still named Dogman's over fifty years later.

Although on this second trip I was the experienced one of the group, I had neglected to plan for a source of fresh water. Since our lodging was at the beach, drinking water was a constant concern. Fortunately, my friend Rodney, who came along on the trip not to surf but to engage with the culture, befriended a local who let us come to the outdoor spigot at his house, fill our jugs with water, and rinse off our salty bodies every few days. It was ironic that the ideal position in the long line for water was last because that was when the water was the coldest; so much for wanting a hot shower! In return, we shared some deluxe American peanut butter with this generous local.

A little bit inland from our beach camp were a few simple wooden homes occupied by local families of modest means. One afternoon, a sweet old woman, who had recently lost her son, invited us to join her for a bowl of soup. We were wary of what to expect, but we knew she needed the company, and we kindly accepted the invitation. She had prepared some kind of stew, which we politely consumed, though a bit nervous about what the dietary consequences might be. We were five young, white, English-speaking surfers from the mainland. She was a seventy-year-old, grey-haired, soft-spoken Puerto Rican woman with missing teeth and a limited understanding of English.

For us, the focus of each day was what the breaks might look like; for her, the focus of each day was dealing with life without her son. She shared a bit about her community and the recent changes, particularly with the influx of surfers. She had never left this rural town and was curious about life in America. We shared a bit about growing up in the '60s in a country with such a high standard of living, but also complex issues. I am not sure who gained more life insights from the conversation. So why, you might wonder, would I remember this single night that happened over fifty years ago? Perhaps because the enormity of our differences did not prevent us from connecting with this old woman with a calming smile. On the surface, we had little in common, but her generosity, combined with our effort to show appreciation, made the evening a lasting memory.

Most of our local interactions were positive ones with a few notable exceptions. Jim and Mary, a stereotypical hippie couple, were drawn to Rincon by the Crosby, Stills, and Nash song "Wooden Ships," not by stories of surf. One evening, they retired early to their tentlike canvas shelter while the rest of us continued to socialize around the fire. Later that night, I looked up from the embers to observe the couple in a romantic embrace when suddenly their shelter unexplainably lifted up and disappeared into the bushes in a matter of seconds. The group around the fire leaped to their feet, and within moments the couple was dressed. Furious, Jim stormed off to town to find the police. No clues to the theft were found that evening, but in the morning Jim found the canvas returned, folded neatly and carefully placed in the adjacent bushes. As we later learned, some of the local fellows were attracted to Mary, but realizing Jim was not appreciative of their interest, they decided to have some fun. They had attached the canvas to one of their horses and galloped off into the fields with it, just a little prank with no harm intended.

Mother Nature graced us with good waves most days, but it wasn't until a week into this trip that the first large swell arrived. The night before, we awoke to what we thought was thunder; however, the sky was clear, and we quickly discerned that the sounds did not come from the sky but the monstrous surf crashing on the reef. The size of the swell was quickly confirmed when we realized the white water was almost up to our sleeping bags. There had been a twenty-foot dry zone in the evening, only a few hours previously, which was now a frothing mass of turbulent white water covering the beach.

Our excitement spiked to the point that sleep was impossible. At dawn, a few of us gathered our boards and walked down the beach to Tres Palmas, the big wave spot that was breaking for the first time on our trip. With hearts pounding as we saw the size of the swells, our first poor decision was to start paddling out without really studying the layout of the break. None of us had ever ridden waves of this size, some close to twenty feet, and our lack of experience proved costly.

Once in the water, approaching the spot where the surf was breaking, it was obvious that the swell was larger than we realized. The three of us got separated as we tried to sense the best place to catch a wave. We each successfully negotiated a few rides, and with my enhanced confidence, I started to cut corners when returning to the takeoff spot. As I paddled back into the lineup after riding a wave, I suddenly saw a cleanup set (a larger-than-normal group of waves that break farther from shore and are more powerful and dangerous) looming on the horizon. I went into high gear, but paddling over the first wave of the set, I realized there was only a slim chance of escaping the ocean's wrath.

There were three more gigantic waves coming my way. When I scratched over the crest of the second one, I sensed I was in serious trouble. I was torn between trying to make it out past the set (away from the beach) or turning around and paddling towards shore, risking the wrath of the white water. Having to make a quick decision, I went with the former plan and got halfway up the front of the next wave when I realized I could not make it over the top to safety. I let go of my board and dove as deeply as I could, but it was too late. With terrific force, the wave swept me backwards, drilling me fifteen feet underwater, tossing me around like a stick in a water fall.

I was held under for far too long, took in a bit of foam as well as salt water, and barely got some air into my lungs before the next wave hit me. Poundings continued as I was washed towards shore, trying to breathe, stay near the surface, and move towards a safe spot. Abandoning my board, my thoughts were only about how to navigate through the coral heads and surging ocean to the one safe exit point on the beach. After being tossed around by a few more waves, I finally found my way out of the water and onto dry sand. I looked back out at the ocean, dizzy from the thrashing, and began to throw up all the salt water that I had ingested. Within a few moments, I regained my composure, only to hear Gary Propper, one of the top surfers in the world, say, "I think I will wait until it calms down a bit before going out." Still processing my experience, my next obvious thought centered on our stupidity in paddling into these huge waves so impulsively.

Within a few minutes, my friends made it to shore. We were all safe but shaken, and I had lost my board. For the next few days, I spread the word about my misadventure and walked the beaches, hoping I would find it washed up on the sand somewhere. As luck would have it, my friend Rodney came through again. He had developed friendships with some of the locals, and one fellow shared that his younger brother had recently found a board just a few miles down the beach. We went to their house, and amazingly enough, there it was, my board! I passed on a few dollars as a thank you and was back in business. The swell did calm down, and the sessions were quite memorable, with lessons learned and all of us being much more cautious after our Tres Palmas calamity.

I have been back to Rincon numerous times over the years, with both friends and family, but camping is no longer an option. The place has developed a great deal and changed significantly, as have I, and as all special places do; but the waves are still there and the memories of the first two visits will remain as some of the most significant ones of my youth.

AUTHOR'S NOTES

Puerto Rico is a tropical island with landscapes varying from dense jungles to arid grasslands. It was first settled by Native Americans around 500 BC and has a complex political history, having been ruled by Spain for 400 years until the United States purchased it after the Spanish-American War in 1898. Since then, it has been a US territory with a controversial set of rights for its population. While Puerto Ricans can travel freely to America, they can participate in the primary but not in the general Presidential election, and they have no Congressional voting representation.

Within the past fifty years, there have been numerous referendums on the status of the island, with the choices being independence, statehood, or the status quo as a territory. Statehood has been receiving the most votes, but any steps to do so have been tied up in Congress for the past decade.

Rincon is on the northwestern coast of the island. It began to develop from a sleepy rural town to a surfing destination after it hosted the World Championships in 1968. There is a deep trench offshore that allows large Atlantic swells to reach its reefs and beaches, which produce excellent surf. The best waves can be found in the fall and winter, and it is known as one of the best surf spots in the entire Caribbean.

The tea cottage

Constructing our lean-to

Harvey at Dogman's

MY ITINERARY | 1976, 1977

I THOUGHT IT WISE TO GIVE THE READER A BRIEF OVER-
view of my two-year trip around the world before sharing some of
my travel stories that follow in this book. Why did I go, and where
was I going . . .

Concerned, I looked at the growing pile of clothes, gear, and
other paraphernalia sprawled across the living room floor. It would
surely fill up two backpacks, and of course, I was only taking one.
What did I need? What did I want? What could I live without for
two years?

I was embarking on a surfing trip around the world. A lifelong
passion, I wanted to see how far I could push myself on my board,
and if not now, it would never happen. While most of my time was
going to be in the tropics, there were a few intended stops in cooler
climates. I knew the South Island of New Zealand could be chilly,
and I wanted to hike in the Himalayas, possibly in the snow. How
could I possibly be prepared for all these climactic zones in one pack?

The other source of my stress was the fact that I really did not
have a plan or, what one might call, an itinerary. My goals were
to surf the best waves in the world, experience other cultures, and
stretch myself. But, where was I going? There were the obvious destinations for any surfer – Hawaii, Australia, Central America – but
I knew there were definitely other spots that had great waves. I just
was not sure where they were.

It was 1976. There was no internet, no way to "search" for the ten best waves in the world. Other than Surfer Magazine, there were no other publications that outlined the prime spots, and even that magazine was reluctant to publicize too many surf breaks, as it would anger the locals.

The movie, "The Endless Summer," which followed two surfers' travels around the world searching for the perfect wave, was part of my inspiration for this trip, but even that only showed about ten locations. Finally, I did not know anyone who had ever taken off on such a trip, so the stress of no roadmap was taking its toll on my excitement for such a venture.

I stared again at the pile on the floor. There were some obvious first cuts. No more than two books; I could obviously pick up additional reads along the way. No binoculars—they would be nice to have, but I realized I needed to get rid of the "nice to haves." Two wetsuits—I could only take one; I went with the Long John as it would double as a pillow or sleeping pad. Did I need a towel? I decided that a bed sheet could be a towel, a sleeping cover when it was too warm to get in a sleeping bag, and a sarong in the hot climates.

The pile began to shrink. It remained on the floor for over a week. Friends passing through would chuckle, give advice, and humorously share their concern about my plan in general, or really, my lack of a plan. A few of them expressed thoughts about ruining my career when I had only three years of teaching behind me.

The final cut included just the essentials. I made peace with deciding what I could purchase along the way vs. what I needed to carry; for example, would I find surfboard wax in Central America? I jammed everything into my pack, and it was manageable. I was at peace with myself, knowing there would be additions and subtractions along the way.

Another important part of my preparation was predicting what this trip would cost. I had saved a few thousand dollars, but since I did not know exactly where I was going, and what the duration of the trip or the expenses might be, I had minimal sense of what funding was needed. I just figured I would go for as long as my savings allowed. As it turned out, my funds were nearly depleted while in New Zealand, but the jobs in Hawaii and Australia allowed me to continue my travels without major financial worries.

As noted several times in the stories, I am known for my Quaker frugality, and at times I erred too much on the cheap side. For example, there were three classes on an overnight ferry to an island off the coast of Thailand with costs ranging from $.50 to $5.00. I chose the cheapest option. As I stepped onto the crowded boat, I saw people laying out their bedding on the expansive deck and figured that it wouldn't be so bad a place to spend the night. Unfortunately when I shared my ticket with a worker, he pointed to an exit for a lower level, and there I was led to a rough, unfinished opening in the floor that sent me down an unstable ladder to a space the size of a football field that was beneath the water line—the home for third class.

My residence for the evening was a smelly, filthy wooden floor filled with what seemed like more chickens, piglets and small goats than people. The sounds and smells made sleep impossible, and I spent most of the night worrying that if this boat started to sink I would be the last one out of the small opening—all for a savings of $4.50.

I was slightly more extravagant with my spending after that evening. I estimated that the entire trip of 18 months cost about $5500, approximately $2000 of which I earned along the way. Reflecting on my expenses for the trip and my reluctance to splurge on anything, nobody should anticipate such a budget today.

Simultaneously, I began to tackle my third major set of decisions: what was my route of travel? My good buddy Doug was joining me, and we agreed to begin the trip by flying out of Miami to Costa Rica. I knew eventually I wanted to go across the Pacific, but other than that, the itinerary was wide open. We decided it was okay just to have plans for the first stop and let the rest fall into place as we progressed.

A high school friend, Chip, my girlfriend, Sherry, and Doug's new wife, Eileen, joined us in Cocoa Beach, and off we went. Our first night in San Jose provided a hint of our inexperience and the adventure to come. We were headed to the tropics, but did not take into account the variable of elevation. San Jose, at 3800 feet, was chilly, and our thin-blooded Florida friends spent their first night of the trip sleeping by the city bus station, shivering. Fortunately, we made it to the coast within two days, and they were once more comfortably warm. This is just one example of how clueless we were.

The exploration of this first country was a bit haphazard and mostly based on conversations with locals. We lived on coconuts, local fruit, and our stock of peanut butter and jelly until it ran out. As time passed, we began to get a bit more creative with our diet and set up beach campsites that had an increasing number of comforts, a place in the shade to read, a source of potable fresh water nearby, for instance. Our time at each locale was usually set by how long the swell lasted or a reaction to a tip someone gave us regarding the merits of another spot.

After a month or so in Costa Rica, our first big decision surfaced—do we head north or south? The lure of South America was enticing for a number of reasons, but our one firm deadline was winter in Hawaii, and since it was getting late in the fall, we feared heading south would make that a challenge. In addition, we had heard promising reports of great waves in El Salvador, so "head north" was the verdict.

That was the right call. After over a month of great waves in El Salvador, we decided on a break from surfing and traveled inland through Guatemala and Mexico, enjoying the historical sites of Palenque, Antigua, Lake Atitlan, Mexico City, as well as some lesser-known destinations.

After these first four months of travel, I had a set rendezvous time with my buddy Tom in Hawaii, so I left my travel companions and headed for the islands. On Maui, we lived out of a rented car, got jobs, and had a magical winter of surfing.

As the winter wound down, we parted ways, and I was on my own with an unclear itinerary. My planned next set stop was New Zealand, but my father had encouraged me to visit some of the smaller Pacific islands, even if the surf forecast for them was nonexistent. Back then, you could purchase a ticket from Hawaii to New Zealand and make three stops without an additional charge. I studied a map and chose Tonga, Western Samoa, and Fiji, as they looked like they had some surfing potential, but I recognized that finding great breaks there was a crapshoot.

Leaving Hawaii by myself, I went on to visit all three of the smaller South Pacific islands, finding surf in two of them. I connected with welcoming, generous locals everywhere, making many fond memories, and landed in New Zealand with seven fellow travelers that I had befriended along the way.

I knew New Zealand had some good waves, but once again, I did not know much about them. Fortunately, on the last leg of the trans-Pacific flights, I observed a fellow reading a New Zealand surfing magazine on the plane, and struck up a conversation. This resulted in him not only telling me where to go, but over the next three months, he took me to a number of spots and served as a tour guide for the whole crew on several occasions. I felt my luck with such matters continued to grow.

My time in New Zealand was in many ways the most enjoyable and fun-filled of the trip, traveling intermittently with my newfound friends on both islands, surfing great breaks, taking some scenic hikes, and exploring an outrageously beautiful country. However, I was getting low on money and was told that one could do much better in Australia, finding work, so I moved on.

Tired of constantly being on the go, I settled in the town of Coolangatta on the New South Wales/Queensland border of Australia, found a construction and restaurant job, and stayed put for a few months. With the arrival of my girlfriend, we hitchhiked up and down the east coast between the Great Barrier Reef and Sydney. Since she was only there for a few months and wanted to see some of the exotic parts of Asia, we went to Bali and Java.

After she returned to the States for work, I traveled on my own up the Malay peninsula and had my eyes opened to some amazing experiences, as I have shared in my stories. The exotic aspects of life in Southeast Asia stretched me on numerous occasions, and the "wow factor" was almost a daily occurrence.

Knowing I would not be near good surf for a while and tiring of lugging a board everywhere, I shipped my 'beloved' from Singapore to Sri Lanka. Traveling without it made life so much easier, but of course, I wondered if I would ever see my board again.

I connected with two Australian travelers in Singapore and stayed with them for the next few months. We parted ways in Nepal, as they had no interest in my desire to hike up into the mountains. Of course, I was not prepared, either. My surf-minded backpack did not include any kind of footwear that would do for such an undertaking, and I went through some interesting hurdles to get appropriate shoes. I could have rented hiking boots from those that the climbers leave after their expeditions, but I could not find the right size. I ended up purchasing a pair of high-top sneakers that were barely satisfactory for the paths we took, but I made my way, nonetheless.

From there, I traveled to India with stops in Agra, Varanasi, New Delhi, and Madras. Each city had its distinct qualities, the Taj in Agra and the intense examples of religious devotion along the banks of the Ganges in Varanasi being the high points. In many ways, this was the most intellectually stimulating portion of the trip, engaging in multiple fascinating conversations with curious locals and witnessing perplexing religious rituals as well as other unique aspects of the country.

My last stop was Sri Lanka, where I retrieved my board and settled into a relaxing few weeks in the small town of Hikkaduwa on the west coast. Unfortunately, as is outlined in the story "The Goodness of People," I contracted hepatitis, ended my trip prematurely, and headed home through India and Poland.

The twists and turns, and the spontaneity of these eighteen months, made for many of the most meaningful experiences of my life, some seemingly magical, others providing a much deeper understanding of the nature and complexity of humanity. Lessons learned that could not have been anticipated in my living room in Philadelphia as I packed, nor planned by any travel agent. I learned to be comfortable with the unknown and unexpected, with no regrets. These were the gifts of my experience.

DANGER AND MISADVENTURES,
COSTA RICA | 1976

WE HAD HEARD THAT A VOLCANO NEAR MARTINIQUE might generate a tidal wave on the East coast of Costa Rica, where we were headed, but that didn't lead us to change our plans. Somehow, we felt confident enough that we could dodge such a wall of water, even though we had never experienced the power of this massive force of nature. The five of us, Chip, Sherry, Doug, Eileen, and I, were looking forward to returning to our life of camping, this time on Punta Cahuita beach, after enjoying a few nights with beds and hot showers in the capital city of San Jose.

To add to the possible tidal wave challenge, I was nursing a strange growth on my leg that developed while I was surfing the wonderful waves of Jaco Beach. It had started out as a minor itch and developed into a nasty-looking wound that was quite painful. A few locals and a doctor in San Jose had given me advice on treatment, but it was not getting better despite my belief that salt water cures anything.

After a scenic train ride through the jungle of eastern Costa Rica filled with exotic animals and plants, followed by a crowded, uncomfortable bus ride down the East Coast, we arrived at the center of the quaint town of Punta Cahuita and went straight to the beach with the first order of business to find a campsite. In our minds, the most important factor of a good location was proximity to the ocean for a quick swim (despite the tidal wave warning confirmed by the locals). We did not err on the side of caution and picked a lovely spot in a coconut grove, only a few yards from the shoreline and a short walk to town.

Doug and I were mildly disappointed with the puny waves, but everyone had snorkeling gear to enjoy the clear waters of the stunning, nearby coral reefs. At the end of our first day in the Caribbean, we wanted to learn more about our new home and knew the best way to do so was at the local bar. Since there was only one in the tiny town, that's where we headed, and we were not disappointed with the lively scene and friendly folks we encountered there.

We connected with several Peace Corps volunteers, who promised to alert us if the tidal wave was coming. They informed us that there was one radio in town that would receive an alert, and if notified, someone would ring the town bell as a call to leave. They said the only people who were really nervous were the Chinese residents, and they had already evacuated. Of course, the Chinese know a lot more about tidal waves than most Americans!

Chip stumbled into a disturbing exchange with a local. The fellow told him there was a good evacuation path up into the mountains, but he was reluctant to describe its location. He said that if Chip tried to find it, he would be waiting with a gun, an odd response that made even Chip a bit uneasy.

Sherry and I struck up a conversation with the owner of the bar, a crusty expat named Warren. He had served in Vietnam as a medic, but could not handle living in the U.S. any longer. His bravado, sense of humor, and vast life experiences made his stories both entertaining and informative. I described the growth on my leg, and he agreed to meet me the next day for treatment. While his brash demeanor was intimidating, I was extremely appreciative of his offer to help me, as I was becoming a bit impatient and nervous about this infection that was not healing. There is always a little extra stress to medical challenges when you are in a foreign country and not familiar with the quality of care you might receive.

There was some question amongst the group about whether I should trust this fellow with my leg, but since there were no alternatives, the next morning I went to Warren's room above the bar for "surgery." His disheveled quarters did not enhance my confidence, but once inside, I knew there was no turning back on his treatment. Warren inspected the wound and quickly diagnosed that there was a pus sack that needed to be removed if I did not want it to infect my entire leg. It was growing inward rather than towards the surface, which complicated matters.

For anesthesia and pain management, "Dr." Warren gave me a good swig of monkey rum and a folded-up leather belt on which to bite. Within minutes, he had removed the puss sack with a hunting knife, and despite the resulting pain, I was on my way to recovery. Warren packed the wound with sulfur and said to keep it as dry as possible for a few days, and all would be well with the leg. I left his room quite sore but cautiously optimistic, believing that I was on my way to recovery, although still a bit worried every time I gazed at the ugly wound.

That same day, Albert, a local lobsterman, struck up a conversation with our crew and invited us to join him for a snorkeling trip the next morning. Albert was one of the real characters in the town, an affable fellow full of insightful, humorous stories about Cahuita, where he had lived his entire life. When the talk turned to the tidal wave, he confidently shared that he had a large balsa log that would be his savior. If the wave was imminent, he would head out to sea in his boat, dive down to a submerged antique cannon, secure one end of a rope to it, and the other end to the log as well as his leg. When the wall of water arrived, he would joyfully ride out the onslaught. We wondered if he really understood the impact of a tsunami or was just a bit crazy, but we were impressed with his bravery and ingenuity, given the circumstances.

The next day was magical. The two-mile hike to Albert's encampment included a beautiful beach and several river crossings, filled with fish and other aquatic animals, and it was clear when we arrived that Albert wanted to make the day special. We loaded our gear into his antique outboard and headed to some colorful reefs to collect lobsters. Even though the Caribbean lobster does not have claws, grabbing the spiny creatures from underneath coral heads was not easy, and the lobster hunt was a source of many laughs and frustrations.

With one breath, one had to dive down about ten feet, spot one of the creatures, usually hidden beneath the coral, sneak up on it, and snag it quickly. There were many returns to the surface empty-handed, but as the morning progressed, so did our successful dives. When Albert declared a sufficient bounty, everyone returned to the boat but me, as I wanted to explore the reef a little more. When I surfaced to share my excitement about a beautiful fish, I heard Doug shout, "Hey Harvey...ya see that fin over there?"

"What?" I sputtered.

"Ya might want to mosey over this way, matey," Doug mused gleefully.

The crew began sharing their excitement about a nurse shark that was gliding between the boat and me. Trying to remain calm, I stroked slowly toward Albert, while periodically scanning the surface for any fins, and fortunately had an uneventful swim to safety.

Upon returning to the camp, Albert began his preparation for the feast by skillfully opening coconuts with his trusty machete and pouring the milk into a large container drum. Meanwhile, the gringos were charged with getting a hot fire going beneath it. Once the liquid started to boil, we threw the lobsters into the milk along with a few fish heads for added flavor. While the crustaceans were cooking, Albert sent a few of us out into the nearby jungle to collect fresh limes. The ensuing feast surpassed any seafood meal at a gourmet restaurant and was accompanied by more nonstop, humorous, insightful stories from Albert about his world. He loved his simple life by the sea and was proud of his ability to make a living from it. However, I did learn later through the grapevine that the reason Albert was giving us all these treats was due in part to his attraction to my girlfriend, Sherry; fortunately, he never went beyond treating us well!

The following days provided each of us with the opportunity to misfire. Mine came first. One of my many flaws is excessive cheapness. As an example, when buying a tent for this trip, I erred on the inexpensive side, and the following evening I paid my dues. We had enjoyed another lovely day of collecting lobsters and imbibed in a tasty meal before settling in for the night. Since we had no access to weather reports, we were completely unaware of the monster storm coming our way. It started with a few drops of rain that quickly turned to a steady downpour, prompting a conversation among the clustered tents. Doug, being much more in tune with the challenges of camping in a thunderstorm and in a better tent, inquired, "Hey, Harvey, how is that tent holding up?"

"Just fine, a little water by the door, but otherwise just ducky!"

A few minutes later …

"Hey, Harvey, seems to be really dumping. I sure hope that cheap tent keeps you comfy! You sure you're not taking in more water?"

"Not yet! Just enjoying getting my feet a bit moist!"

Sherry, not quite as willing to be waterlogged as I was, added, "Hey, Doug, you have any room at the inn?"

While trying to save face with Doug, I could feel the floor of the tent go from a little dampness by our feet, to a small puddle, to so much water that the bottom of our sleeping bags started to feel increasingly moist. Within a few minutes, our tent was soaked, and Doug was having a ball continuing his questions with loud chuckles in between. Suffice it to say, the quality of sleep that night varied!

The next day was Chip's misadventure. Having gained a reputation as the best cook in the group, Chip decided he was going to create a special bean dish. Nobody had eaten much that day, so we were really looking forward to his gourmet concoction. He had procured some fresh veggies and seasoning from the local market and mixed them with the beans in our one large pot. As the ingredients began to cook, the aroma enhanced our hunger and anticipation of a great meal. Not having a great deal of fresh water, resourceful Chip decided to use ocean water, and when the water boiled out, he simply added more, not realizing that while the water disappeared, the salt remained. To our dismay, we had a hard time arriving at the realization that we had to throw out the entire meal. Due to the extraordinary amount of salt in it, Chip's vegetable stew was inedible, even for this group, who had a low bar for our cuisine.

Next, it was Doug and Eileen's turn. One of the challenges of living out of a tent is the issue of security. Where do you put your valuables when you are out in the water all day? Chip, Sherry, and I, being from Philadelphia, were more paranoid than our friends from Florida, and we came up with the idea of burying the most critical items in the sand. Each morning, we would choose a different spot near the tents, fill a bag with what we thought needed hiding, dig a hole with a makeshift shovel, and camouflage the spot with a little brush.

Doug and Eileen, having more faith in humanity, thought this chore was a waste of time and left everything in their tent. Upon returning from a swim one day, to their dismay, followed by fury and helplessness, they discovered some of their belongings were missing: his prized knife, binoculars, some sandals, along with a few other items. Doug was steaming, declaring, "Somebody in this town is going to pay for this!"

That evening, a series of events at a dance in town at the local bar restored our faith in humanity. Everyone in Punta Cahuita from five to eighty was there, and a positive spirit filled the air. Of course, Albert was in attendance, and Doug shared the news about the stolen belongings with him. About an hour later, Albert took Doug aside and said that if he followed the barbed wire along the second path to the right, on the dirt road back to our campsite, and dug around the third palm tree, he would find all the missing items. We all followed Albert's directions with a combination of suspicion and excitement.

The task was made easier thanks to the blessing of a full moon, but we still found the route a challenge, as the paths were covered with a variety of roots, causing a few minor trips. It was quite a sight, the five of us mumbling our misgivings to each other as we stumbled along the path without flashlights. To our astonishment, when we rustled amongst the fronds at the base of the third tree, there were Doug's "lost" possessions!

This was the ultimate example of the unique, generous spirit of Punta Cahuita, but there were other moments when locals were so helpful to us. Napoleon, an Indian fellow, climbed trees, procuring coconuts for our lobster dinners on the beach. Bernardo, a local kid, brought us oranges and, with his machete, helped us build our "cabana."

The tsunami never materialized, and the lessons learned stayed with us:

- Don't buy a cheap tent
- Don't cook with salt water
- Hide your goodies when camping
- Always keep your faith in humanity

AUTHOR'S NOTES

Punta Cahuita is a small town on the southeastern Caribbean coast of Costa Rica. It was a destination for us for a variety of reasons. We were there in September, as the weather is much more pleasant than on the Pacific coast during the rainy season (May-October). In addition, this coast picks up the Caribbean hurricane swells, which makes for good surfing. Finally, the nearby national park is a popular destination for ecotourists.

The beach camping was fantastic, but it was the diversity of people that made the experience special. In 1976, Cahuita was a small town with just a bar and a market surrounded by about thirty homes with other residences further out on the beach and in the jungle. As with most of the places we visited, the small-town feel is gone, and it is now a full-blown resort with hotels, restaurants, and many rental homes.

Garnering wisdom from the locals

Albert and the Lobster Crew

CROSSING BORDERS,

GUATEMALA AND MEXICO | 1976

CARRYING OUR SURFBOARDS AND BACKPACKS IN THE withering heat was not easy during the mile-long trek from the bus depot in Northern Guatemala to the border, and we were hopeful that crossing into Mexico would be a brief process. It had been a long day's journey, and Doug, Eileen, and I were eager to get to a town and some sense of comfort. Our hopes diminished slightly when we saw up ahead on the border a dilapidated shack with a small hand-painted sign "cruce de frontera (Border Crossing)." Maybe the process would not be as brief as we had hoped, as the complex did not emanate substantial legitimacy.

When we entered the hut, a slovenly-clad, elderly woman slowly creaked from her chair and shuffled to the counter. We let Eileen begin the engagement with this official because she spoke fluent Spanish and was part Mexican. All of us had been to this country many times in our travels, and we knew that the only necessary document for entry was a tourist card that could be obtained at the border, if not beforehand. Doug and Eileen had smartly secured theirs in Huehuetanango, but I had gone off to climb a volcano for a few days and not taken that precaution.

My friends easily completed their paperwork, but when I began my transaction, I was informed that there were no tourist cards here, and to get one, I would have to return to Huehuetenango, an eight-hour bus ride away. That was not going to happen. I knew the drill of sharing a few pesos to solve most problems in Mexico, and I offered the alternative plan of me purchasing one. The smile on her face not only assured me that I would get through the border but also infuriated me that this step, bordering on bribery, was necessary to complete the routine process.

I decided that I needed to take a stand of some kind, and just then she placed a card on the counter which said in English: "It is requested that you give us a donation for the extra work involved in completing your papers." It is important to note that this was a border between two Spanish-speaking countries, and no English was spoken during our exchange. My anger surged when I saw her open a drawer and take a tourist card from a large stack. That was the "extra work!" Impulsively, I arrived at a plan. I always carry some American currency with me when I am in foreign countries, so I displayed some bills, which in turn sped up the process and widened the smile on her face. However, once I had the papers in hand, I reached into my pocket, put a few leftover coins from El Salvador on the counter (which were virtually worthless), quickly packed up my gear, and exited the building amidst a barrage of her Spanish curses.

Once outside, I eagerly shared my immigration exploit with Doug and Eileen, and the three of us began our lengthy trek to the nearest town. The heat continued to tire us, and the barren landscape showed little sign of human or animal life except for the occasional scrubby bushes growing out of the parched earth. We walked for about a mile with not much to distract us from our conversation, when suddenly out of a thicket emerged two men claiming to be agricultural inspectors. They were dressed in makeshift uniforms, brandished rifles, reeked of alcohol, and emanated little semblance of police status. They asked us to empty our packs, and we reluctantly complied, knowing we were not bringing anything illegal into the country.

Although we were veterans of nerve-racking experiences with officials in Mexico, we were unsure how this encounter would proceed.

Years before, on a surfing trip to Mazatlan, I was warned never to let a Mexican official inspect my pocket without inserting my hand into it, as they might slip in something illegal. This tip was helpful because almost immediately on that trip, we were checked by "una agente federale." When he went to put his hand in my pocket, I quickly slipped mine in first and emptied it, watching nervously as he pulled away with a bag of pot in his. Seeing that we were onto his tricks, he let us go.

On the same trip, we got into a verbal altercation with some local boxers in a seaside bar. Sensing disaster coming, we knew there were police outside the establishment and went to ask for help. However, before we knew what happened, our adversaries went outside and asked the cops to take a walk around the block, so they could thrash us. We only escaped by frantically jumping into a passing pickup truck and paying the driver to speed off! These are just two examples of our experiences south of the border that heightened our "antennas of concern" whenever engaging with any Mexican government official.

So, as our current luggage search by the "agricultural inspectors" was going slowly, we sensed trouble was brewing. One of the men made a feeble attempt to take Doug's beloved hammock, but was met with a clear negative response. The other fellow was eyeing my air mattress that displayed an ad for Black Velvet whisky with a beautiful woman on it. Not being extremely attached to the item, I felt sacrificing the mattress was a way out of this ordeal. I said something to the effect that my pack was too full; I really didn't use the mattress that much, and wondered if he would like it. Fortunately, parting with the air mattress was our partial ticket to an exit from this awkward brush with the "inspectors."

As the bizarre exchange continued, and our frustration was

mounting, a local bus was slowly passing by, and the driver, sensing immediately what was transpiring, stopped, opened the doors, and in an authoritarian tone told us to get in. While carefully eyeing the irritated reactions of the "officials," we gladly obliged and escaped the nuisance of these characters, who were watching somewhat helplessly as we exited. Obviously, there was more to this relationship between the driver and the inspectors than we knew. It was a great reminder of the goodness of many Mexicans, particularly when challenges surface.

Once we were safely away from the scene, the driver let us out of the bus. We expressed our gratitude, packed up our gear once more, and headed for town, glad to be past that hurdle. I wondered if somehow the immigration lady had gotten word to these other "officials" or if it was just their way of passing the time and gaining some treasures from traveling gringos.

Luck seemed to be with us, for just as we arrived in town, the bus to our destination, the ancient Mayan ruins of Palenque, was preparing to depart. In addition, this vehicle was relatively clean with no foul odors, had comfortable seats, and was not overcrowded, all of which was uncommon for Latin American buses. We quickly threw our boards and packs in the luggage compartment underneath the coach and settled into relative comfort for the next few hours, picking up on some much-needed sleep.

It was early evening when we arrived at the town square in San Cristóbal de las Casas, and we were a bit groggy from our naps. Doug happened to look out the bus window and erupted when he saw someone grab Eileen's pack from the luggage compartment and take off down the street. We exited the bus quickly, creating as much commotion as possible, and raced to retrieve her pack, but lost track of the thieves amongst the crowds within minutes. Locals seemed to want to help us, but being gringos was an obvious liability. Doug was furious, and we wondered, since Eileen's pack and mine looked similar, whether we were still paying the price for my antics at the border?

Naturally, the unfortunate series of events gave me pause for my actions. On the one hand, is it right for Americans to be viewed as human wallets and taken advantage of as they travel and cross borders? On the other hand, the woman at the crossing was most likely paid very little, and a few dollars meant a lot more to her than they did to me. I felt a bit torn by my reaction to the problem, especially if it cost Eileen her pack.

Despite our upsetting encounters with the "official" at the border and the "agricultural inspectors" on the road, as well as the loss of Eileen's pack, we were a resilient crew. In a single day, we pieced together replacements for most of her possessions, recognizing that other than a few mementos, the stolen items had some value but no real meaning in her life. It was a hassle to go through replacing some things, and there was a sense of violation, but it was temporary. Nonetheless, I continued to have a nagging feeling that my actions at the border may have been the cause of all these misfortunes.

The next day, we moved on to the ruins of Palenque, and soon the theft was just a good story. Doug set us on a memorable path when, as we were walking to the ruins from town, he strolled through a field full of cattle, picked some mushrooms from a few of their "poop pies," and convinced us that eating them would make for a better day. I shared my skepticism regarding the safety of eating these bits of fungi, but Doug, being familiar with similar ones in Florida, noted the purple band around their trunks as a sign that they were safe to eat. Showing our trust in him, we consumed the mushroom, and a fascinating day in the ruins ensued, a great way to forget our border challenges.

In my trip around the world that year, I estimated that I crossed approximately forty international borders with very few challenges, but after this harrowing experience, there is always an uptick in my blood pressure when I approach an official, remembering our adversity at the Mexican frontier. I often take a second look at any border agent, wondering how they perceive their role in dealing with travelers.

How do they balance their power and responsibility to their country, alongside empathy for the tourists they are serving? I also wonder if that placard is still in use on the counter in Mexico and whether my air mattress is still being enjoyed in some nearby home.

AUTHOR'S NOTES

The stress of border crossings varies immensely. However, I have learned a few tricks that help take the stress out of the process. I try to have what I call my "customs costume," a set of clean, somewhat formal clothes. This can be challenging on a lengthy surfing trip, but I always managed to have at least one unwrinkled collared shirt. Also, I wear slacks, if not, nice-looking shorts, and shoes that cover my feet. I always try to look in a mirror before approaching a crossing to comb my hair and ensure that my persona is as well-kept as possible.

In terms of interaction with the border guards, I've learned to be pleasant but not chatty, look them in the eyes, and not seem nervous, even if I am. As with any human interaction, I try to put myself in their shoes. And lastly, I try to have all my papers in order and easily accessible.

As for my gear, even if everything is stuffed in a backpack, I take the time to fold it nicely, making it easy to search. Obviously, if I have any questionable items, food, souvenirs, etc., I ask about them before they are found.

If there is a challenge of some kind, I do not resist the official's actions. For example, I watched a customs officer in Malaysia stick a pin in my surfboard to make sure it was not filled with drugs! I did not make a scene, as the hole was easy to repair and not worth the repercussions of a confrontation.

The story here is about Mexico, which has a crossing that is potentially stressful and is listed as one of the top ten most dangerous borders in the world. The combination of the immigration issue, the popularity of Mexico as an inexpensive travel destination, and the economic disparity between the two countries combine to make the border a potential source of tension. While one needs to be ready for a challenge, it is important to note that most of the Mexican officials are honest, helpful, and hardworking.

There are some other borders that can also be stressful for a variety of reasons. Singapore has some of the harshest customs regulations. I remember flying there for the first time and having the flight attendant announce that the discovery of drugs on any visitor can be punishable by death. You can't even bring chewing gum into that country.

Obviously, at any border, I try to be aware of the relationship between the two countries, particularly if there is any political conflict or tension between them. As with anything I do in life, I try to do my homework before crossing into a country, learning as much as I can about what to expect. It is worth the effort.

LOCALISM: HAWAII, WESTERN SAMOA, COSTA RICA, NEPAL, EL SALVADOR | 1976-77

THE WAVES AT MAKAHA WERE PERFECT, BIG ENOUGH to give you a thrilling, long ride, but not "Hawaiian scary." We only had one board between us, and Tom graciously gave me the first shot in the lineup. As I stroked out through the waves, focusing on the incoming swells, I did not notice the surfer paddling directly towards me. The gigantic fellow suddenly clenched the nose of my board as he approached, and uttered with a chuckle, "Haole boy, you take off on my wave, I punch your lights out." He smiled, pushed my board away, and stroked to the lineup. After I gathered my senses, I realized he was Ben Aipa, a strapping local who had the body of a defensive lineman and was one of the top big wave surfers in the world.

I had some beautiful rides that day, but with each take off, I had the extra challenge of ensuring that neither Ben nor his friends were interested in the same wave. During the lulls, my mind was con-sumed with the fact that I was the only "haole," or foreigner, in the water. Surrounded by competent, edgy Hawaiians, I pondered "localism," where those who grew up here have priority over main-land "intruders" like me. Having surfed in the Hawaiian breaks for the past few months, I was well aware of the tensions between the locals and mainland haoles, but this was my first experience being the lone "outsider" in the lineup.

Everybody is a local of some kind, connected with the natural wonders, geography, ethnic makeup, population, or history and culture of their birthplace. This sense of "ownership," where local people and culture are prioritized, varies in intensity. If you have lived in a number of different places, this feeling of roots may not be that important. However, if your family has resided for generations in the same locale, and you have spent most of your life there, the intensity of your localism may be far greater. That feeling is often even deeper if there is a significant amount of outsider contact with tourists and other visitors, which can be disruptive to one's daily routine. One only has to listen to the news of the "anti-tourist" demonstrations in Europe during the Summer of 2025 to understand this reality.

Hawaii is a great example of the delicate relationship between locals and visitors. For centuries, the Hawaiian Islands have attracted people from all over the world for obvious reasons. Despite efforts to maintain the "aloha" ethos, the influx of travelers and other new arrivals, coupled with its political evolution, has impacted the islands significantly, and many of the native Hawaiians resent these changes.

To put this idea in surfing terms, there are a finite number of great waves that grace Hawaiian beaches each year, and the tension between the locals and non-islanders competing for the waves is totally understandable. The local population watches plane loads of surfers from all over the world arrive each winter and compete with them for rides on what they consider their waves. I was obviously one of those "out-of-towners."

Surfing has given me the most concrete example of localism. I am from Avalon, New Jersey, and have enjoyed the waves there since 1963. Even at seventy-five, I rarely paddle out at my home break without running into someone I know, and it is very natural to give a wave to a friend. I feel a strong connection to this stretch of beach and cringe a bit when it gets crowded with people I do not know.

Traveling a few miles in either direction from this break, my comfort level and sense of "home" slightly diminishes with a decreased feel for the surf patterns and connection with the surfers who ride the waves there.

There are places that have the reputation of "if you don't live here, don't surf here." For example, locals might wear a certain color wetsuit, so they know when outsiders arrive and treat them accordingly. The most extreme examples lead to fights in the water or the destruction of property.

As a point of contrast from Hawaii, Western Samoa is a geographically similar tropical South Pacific gem; yet it does not have as much contact with foreigners, as it is further away from major population centers. The reception of haoles in Western Samoa couldn't be more different from Hawaii. Locals want to show you their good surf breaks and often go a step further, inviting you to stay in their homes. I did not see many other surfers there during my visit, though I did find some fine waves, and whenever I exited the water, there was usually a group of friendly local kids eager to try my board and show me around the beach. They were generally curious about me and the sport I loved, and eager to make a good impression as well as a new friend.

I was with two Canadians when I traveled to Samoa, and within twenty-four hours of our arrival, a local girl by the name of Hilder had taken us under her wing, gladly showing us the island and insisting that we stay with her family. I have never felt so welcomed into a community. Her father was the chief of the village, and as we walked the paths amongst the homes which had no walls, families would wave to us and engage in friendly conversations. At meals, we were asked to eat first and were fanned by a few of Hilder's twenty-five siblings to keep us cool and the flies at a distance.

As an extreme example of their hospitality, her family wanted to cook us a special meal, and they heard Americans like red meat. Sadly, not having cattle locally, they killed one of their dogs and served it to us. We simultaneously expressed our appreciation and forced ourselves to digest the chewy dish, not wanting to be honest about our feelings regarding eating dog and offend them.

This island, unlike Hawaii, has not had a major influx of foreign interaction, and seemingly, the potential for possible negative aspects of localism is minimal. The only real tension I personally observed involved the arrival of a number of football recruiters from the U.S. The Samoans are extremely large and have the potential to become great athletes on the gridiron, but some mothers whom we met were concerned about how their child's experience in America might change their wholesome spirit. If one looks at NFL rosters today, one will see evidence that a number of these recruiters convinced them otherwise.

In my travels over four decades, I have observed a country evolve from the spirit of Western Samoa to that of Hawaii and witnessed an understandable rise of localism as a result. Costa Rica, a unique Latin American nation, refuses to have an army, has one of the highest percentages of land devoted to national parks in the world, and is known for its sense of peace, unlike its neighbors. It also has two coastlines filled with great surf spots. I have been going there since the mid-'70s and have noticed a slow change in this extraordinary nation as it became a more complicated international society, impacted by the influx of foreigners, some on vacation and others as new residents.

In the '70s, Tamarindo Beach was a quiet town on the Northwest Pacific coast, populated by local fishermen, farmers, and a few itinerant surfers. The center of town was nothing more than a few homes, restaurants, and stores on a dirt road facing a long sandy beach. Right in the center of town, there were a few old school buses that served as shelter for some of the surfers.

On this first visit, there were only a few established local surfers. My buddies, Doug and Chip, were camping on the beach with me and surfing right out in front of the parked buses. It is commonplace to ask veteran surfers about the "best local spots," and some folks are more forthcoming than others. After a few days of uninspired surfing in town, one of the old timers spilled the beans. There was a secret spot a half mile down the beach, which you could not see from town. You had to follow a path through the jungle to the mouth of a river. On our first visit to the secret spot, known as Langusta, we enjoyed some terrific waves with just the three of us in the water. The tip from a local took us from mild disappointment with the surf to the joy of finding a true "aquatic treasure."

Tamarindo was later featured in the movie, *Endless Summer Two*, and that exposure, coupled with the discovery of other local attractions such as fishing and white-water rafting, turned this special spot into a full-scale resort for foreign travelers with many fancy hotels and all the other tourist draws such as bars and nightclubs. Before long, Americans began to purchase second homes, and, needless to say, the quaint beach town of Tamarindo is no more. Gone are the secret spots, where you can surf with just a few friends.

Pavones, also in Costa Rica, is known for having one of the finest point breaks on the planet. It is similarly located on the Pacific near the Panamanian border. Doug, one of my original surf buddies from the '70s, purchased a home near Pavones, just outside of town, so I visited there frequently. While challenging to get to, as early as the '80s, the local campgrounds, budget hotels, and restaurants accommodated many surfers from all over the world.

When the waves were good, it became increasingly difficult to navigate the crowds, but Doug learned of a number of nearby breaks that had not been discovered by the masses. We guarded the identity of one break as best we could, promising we would never tell anyone its name or location. We had to drive to it, and when we turned off the main road to its entrance, we would make sure no cars saw us as we sped down the first portion of the side road to keep it to ourselves. We parked at the end of the dirt stretch and walked about a mile to a phenomenal spot that, for a number of years, was never crowded.

Here in this cherished place, I felt like a local despite being nothing more than an infrequent visitor. I passionately wanted to keep this place secret to preserve the magic of surfing great waves with just a few others in the water. But the obvious truth was that I, too, was one of the many coming to this special place that was not "mine"; I was not a local, just a fortunate outsider.

After a day of great surfing at Pilon, we would often go into Pavones for dinner and listen to friends complain about the crowds at the main break. They would ask where we had been all day, and we would respond with the untruth that we had not surfed or gone to one of the known other breaks, never mentioning our secret spot. Over time, however, the word got out, and the crowds arrived. The magic of this break is gone forever. The last time I went, I got into an altercation with a surfer from California and had to battle for waves as one must at most known great spots.

The evolution of these two areas and my reaction to the changes highlight the complexities of localism. Is it okay to lie to friends and purposely withhold information to preserve the special elements of a locale? How do you respond to a place that you once loved for its simplicity, which is now more crowded, expensive, and lacking the wonderful ethos it once had? In the end, Doug and I felt it was more important to preserve the special elements of our secret spot than to tell the truth about where we had surfed. We knew that once an unknown break was discovered, there was no going back. It would be forever changed.

As one engages with different local cultures, there are often "teachable moments." I once witnessed a classic mistake made by a fellow hiker in a remote region of the Himalayas in Nepal. There were a few small groups of trekkers who were walking from village to village in an area that seemed to be from the Middle Ages, so far removed from life as we knew it in the States. The routine on this trek was to be on the trails most of the day, arrive at a village in the evening, stay with a family who would offer dinner along with a sleeping mat, breakfast, and some snacks for the next day's trek. The accommodations were primitive, and the food was based on local availability, dahl baht (Nepalese lentil curry) for most. Trekkers would usually pay for the food and shelter with items not available in the village. For example, we were carrying a huge chunk of cheese and would give each family a piece along with some other supplies such as toothpaste and Band-Aids.

We were traveling at the same pace as a British group of hikers, one of whom would give balloons to every child in each village she visited. I watched the exchange a few times and saw some negative consequences of this well-intentioned gesture. The normal "toys" of the village children were all made from local materials. If a toy broke, it could easily be replaced. Balloons, on the other hand, could not, and invariably a few would explode, and the issue of the "haves" and the "have-nots" caused tension amongst the children. By the time we arrived at the fifth village, I explained my observations to the woman who gave the children balloons.

She immediately understood that she had not thought about the consequences of her actions and terminated the gesture, recognizing the importance of honoring the local customs, products, and traditions.

While living in the town of Sunzal, El Salvador, we befriended two surfers from Texas who had arrived with a pickup truck full of toys: surfboards, diving gear, bicycles, and motorbikes. While these two fellows provided lots of enjoyable moments, they were inexperienced travelers and tended to act before thinking through potential consequences. Unfortunately, there were a number of instances in which they did not understand the realities of visiting a country quite different from the U.S. One afternoon, they mindlessly lent their motorbikes to two young locals. One boy, who had never driven one previously, lost control of the bike, drove it off a bridge, and was tragically killed. The people of the small, rural community were understandably heartbroken. While relations with the international surfers up until then were positive for the most part, friends and family of the boy were outraged at the fellows from Texas who were responsible for such a tragedy, and there was a resulting uptick in the tension between the locals and visitors.

The response was swift. Police arrived, impounded all of the Texans' gear, and took them off to jail. My friend Doug and I were also outraged, but well aware of the complications for Americans being arrested in this country. We had a thoughtful conversation with a local whom we trusted, who confirmed our concerns. We needed to get them out of jail and out of the country as soon as possible because justice in El Salvador would be challenging for them. Doug contacted their family in Texas and had them wire us money. We went to the police station and, with our most tactful demeanor, gave the police a few hundred dollars for bail.

The surfers were released, but their main concern was getting all their belongings back. Doug, with his strong Floridian tone, was clear with them. "Forget about your gear; get your asses out of this country, now!"

They argued weakly against that plan, but within hours, they were on their way to Mexico. By the time they crossed the border, they were thankful that Doug had been so adamant about the path forward, and later on, thanked him personally for all that we had done for them. We did our best to grieve with and soothe the community after such a tragedy, but that process needed to be the work of the Salvadorians, not the visiting American surfers. There were wounds in our relationship with the locals as a result of the Texan's stupidity, which hopefully time would heal. Many of these people had become our close friends. This hard lesson left a strong impression on us about the importance of thoughtful engagement with people of other cultures.

I learned from my mistakes and observations of other travelers to be a better, more respectful visitor and to honor the ways of different homelands. From then forward, I always surveyed the lineup before I paddled out, so to speak. I still might bump into a Ben Aipa, so I stay away from his waves, but I don't let him stop me from getting a few of my own!

AUTHOR'S NOTES

The areas mentioned in this piece include Hawaii, Western Samoa, New Jersey, Nepal, El Salvador, and Costa Rica. The background for Hawaii, El Salvador, and Costa Rica is sufficiently described in this story, and El Salvador is discussed in the introduction.

Avalon, New Jersey, is a beach town on a barrier island along the Atlantic coast. Its population swells in the summer but is very quiet from October to May. It is where I learned how to surf and is still my home break.

There are two Samoan Islands in the middle of the Pacific Ocean. American Samoa is the southernmost territory of the United States, which took control of it in the late 1800s to establish a naval outpost. Western Samoa, known officially as Samoa since 1991, is an independent country since 1961, though Germany, the United States, Great Britain, and New Zealand all made efforts to control it. Settled by Polynesians thousands of years ago, its remoteness has allowed it to develop without a great deal of foreign interference despite some contact with missionaries and various economic interests. The author, Robert Louis Stevenson, resided there and made it known through his writings.

Sandwiched between India and China, Nepal is an independent country, known for its mountains with eight of the ten highest peaks in the world within its borders.

They are a draw for climbers from all over the world, making tourism central to its economy. While the majesty of nature there is spectacular, the Buddhist influence evident in the temples and other religious sites, and mountain village life provide insights into this fascinating insular nation.

A final example concerning localism.

Tourist Review of Makaha Beach Park on TripAdvisor:

Nice Beach Unfriendly Locals, 1 October 2015

Spent an afternoon quietly enjoying the beach, we were unobtrusive and respectful, but obviously white and not Hawaiian…sorry not super tan!! Sad to find a note on our car indicating Locals Only were welcome at this beach.

Left a bad taste in my mouth. Didn't feel good about spending money on "their Island" or supporting their local economy. I also live in a tourist community and recognize the contribution and welcome visitors.

Our home without walls with our host children

Ben Aipa, my greeter and companion at Makaha

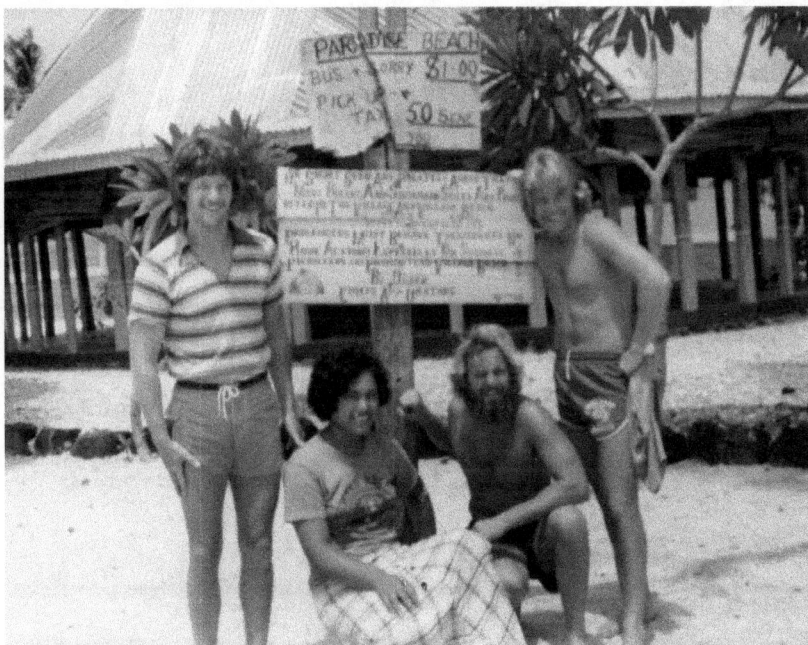

Lindsay, Bob, and I posing with our tour guide, Hilder. The sign says: On sight seen are politely asked that mini bikinis and swimming suits are prohibited in the village and village beach. Beach speed 10 mph. Passengers must behave themselves. No rude actions especially on Sundays. Picnickers are prohibited from the village beach—By Order of Chiefs and Orators

Curious, friendly Samoan locals engaging with "Papalagi"

HAWAIIAN WINTER | 1976-77

━━━━━━━━━━

AS I STEPPED OFF THE PLANE AT THE AIRPORT ON MAUI, I was relieved to see Tom's smiling face in the waiting area. It is always so uplifting to have a friend meet you when you arrive at a new place. I was three months into my round-the-world trip and anxious to spend time with my old buddy, a veteran of many adventures, and finally surf the waves of Hawaii. When I began to plan my itinerary for my surfing journey, Hawaii was on the must-do list.

For a football player, the ultimate dream is to play in the Super Bowl, to a climber, it is Mt Everest, to a surfer in the 1970s, it was to surf the waves of Hawaii at their winter peak. As I learned the sport in my teens, I saw pictures in magazines and shots in movies of these amazing waves and dreamed of someday having the chance, skill, and confidence to ride them. Now it was happening, and I nervously hoped I was up to the challenge.

We were staying with Tom's high school friend, Phil, on a funky plot of land near the 'upcountry' town of Makawao, located in the verdant hills on the eastern side of the island. His compound included the small artsy home he shared with his girlfriend, Rita, an impressive garden along with an orchard of a number of native fruit-bearing trees, a rundown shed which Tom and I turned into our sleeping quarters, and, most importantly, the furrow. This was an antiquated hot tub made out of redwood with a copper covering around the bottom and fueled by a wood fire, which we would build an hour or so before we wanted to get wet. It was the gathering spot for the community and a great way to relax your muscles after a session in the waves.

Like me, Phil had decided to go on a surf trip around the world. His first stop was Maui, and he never left. This is totally understandable given the beauty of the island, the lifestyle, and the great waves. The one challenge with settling there is the high cost of living, but Phil did quite well with what he called his chores. He had an impressive "green thumb" and developed a remote plot on the nearby, sparsely populated island of Molokai, a former leper colony, where he grew a potent strain of marijuana called Maui Wowie. He sold most of his harvest to a famous rock star for $75,000. That transaction, coupled with a small sailing charter business, took care of most of his expenses for the year.

On our first surfing excursion, Phil shared some of his bounty with us, and its strength, coupled with the power of the waves, made for a frightening introduction to the Hawaiian surf. We paddled out through the channel at a nearby point that allowed us to get to the takeoff spot without having to go through the intimidating breakers. The surf in Hawaii is powerful. In the winter, storms formed in the Arctic push down massive swells that break on the north-facing reefs of the islands. A six-foot wave in Hawaii has the force of a ten-footer on the East Coast.

That first afternoon, I was a nervous Hawaiian rookie in the water, intimidated by the power of the waves and wanting to prove myself with my new friends. I was very careful to choose the smaller waves of the sets and paddle in the channel to return to the takeoff spot rather than take the shortcut through the massive breakers. From then on, I declined Phil's offer before entering the water. I needed to have my wits about me to surf here.

After the first week, Tom and I landed a job with Duke Boyd, an old-time big wave surfer, who ran a nursery perched on a beautiful hillside overlooking the ocean. While Duke didn't surf anymore, he loved to "talk story" about his many adventures. He was very understanding of our priorities, and when we would look out and see the swell picking up, he would smile and say it was time to quit for the day, so we could catch some waves.

Makawao was a dynamic village with a diverse collection of characters. Tom had befriended a Zen Buddhist leader, the world's foremost white roshi, at an enchanting, nearby zendo (a Buddhist meditation retreat). The lush complex included a number of ornate Buddhist buildings amidst the colorful gardens. We would occasionally visit this beautiful compound and "sit" with the roshi and some of the devotees.

The first time we went, Tom said to simply follow his lead while in a meditative position facing the walls of a small, beautiful temple. When I saw Tom raise his hands slowly, I did the same, but was shocked when a priest came over and gently struck my back with a keisaku, known as a stick of encouragement. Raising one's hands was a sign of a need for redirection, but nobody had warned me of what that meant. After an initial negative reaction to the unique treatment, I settled back into my relaxed state, wanting not to create any more commotion amongst the calm, focused gathering.

The roshi was a wise, mellow man who was curious about Quakerism. After our "sittings," we engaged in lengthy discussions comparing my faith to Buddhism, both of us gaining fascinating insights from the exchange.

Christmas was approaching, and my girlfriend Sherry arrived along with my travel mates, Doug and Eileen. Being too many people for Phil's shed, we rented a car and began to explore the island. Honolua Bay became our favorite spot. The spectacular point break beneath large cliffs, with the small island of Molokai as a backdrop, and whales often passing by offshore, made for an idyllic place to spend the day. The only downside was the number of surfers who had the same idea – the crowds were a challenging variable. With the intensity of the break and beautiful long rides, everyone in the water was accomplished and eager to catch as many waves as possible, even if it meant cutting other surfers off. You had to be aggressive if you wanted to get a good ride.

For someone unfamiliar with surfing, it is important to understand this challenge. It is always best to look carefully at an unfamiliar spot before you paddle out and get a sense of where the best waves are breaking. In the case of Honolua, one also had to figure out how to get into the water at the base of the cliffs and find a safe path to the waves.

I usually try to be the farthest out in the lineup, where I can best see the incoming sets. At a surf break of Honolua's caliber, there will often be numerous surfers paddling for the same wave. The etiquette is to give the wave to the first person standing or the one closest to the curl, but unfortunately, that is not always followed, and tensions can develop. You need to establish yourself as a surfer who is going to take off on the best waves and ride them successfully, which requires paying extremely close attention to where they are breaking. We were getting our share of these tremendous waves until I had a run-in with the reef that resulted in numerous stitches in my forehead and a few days out of the water.

When our friends left after Christmas, Tom and I went back to work, landing a job at the Treehouse restaurant in Lahaina, with our first night on the job being a hectic New Year's Eve. Located right on the esplanade facing the ocean, the seating included tables on platforms amidst the strong branches of a beautiful banyan tree. The work crew was an eclectic community of characters. There was a delightful hula show multiple times each evening, though the dancers were all from Chicago, who wowed the crowd with their moves and kept us laughing with their sense of humor in between performances.

My boss was a bizarre fellow we nicknamed "terrible Terry." Functioning on steady doses of various drugs, he turned out great dishes but ran a chaotic kitchen. There was a window between the cooking and dishwashing area, and one night, he threw a hot, greasy frying pan through the opening, hitting a dishwasher, who summarily threw it back at him. A brief but intense altercation ensued, with the result being a subsequent less frenetic ethos to the work environment.

Handsome Tom was a waiter, and my role evolved from dishwasher to second cook. With little kitchen experience, I just took directions from Terry; however, he gave me some freedom with the soups. Though probably not up to health code, I often took some of the leftovers to make a base for them and was known for some crazy concoctions for which I would give unique names, such as "Cruzan Confusion."

Tom and I had to make a decision about how to deal with housing and transportation, and we went with renting an old, rusty station wagon for $140 a month. We wanted to be able to get around to all the surf breaks and gambled that since there were enough beaches to sleep on, we didn't need to rent an apartment. At least once a week, Tom would charm some customers at the restaurant to invite us back to their condo or home, which provided more comfort for sleeping, the use of a fridge, and a good shower.

Our most frequented sleeping locale was a beach at the base of Honolua Bay. There were a number of other surfers who made that spot home, and there was an interesting collection of improvised sleeping quarters on the small beach and surrounding woods. We were popular with the crew as we would collect all the leftovers from the restaurant and arrive after closing with the treats for our friends there. There was one excellent surfer from California, whom we called "bitchin' mellow," as they were his descriptor for virtually everything. He had run out of money but wanted to stay on Maui to ride the great waves and would consume a number of our cold baked potatoes as his only real meal of the day.

There were other creative sources of food that winter. A sizable, but diminishing portion of Maui is covered by pineapple fields. Tom was aware that after the harvest, the fields were left alone for a few months, and invariably, there was a lot of wasted fruit. When the time was right, we drove our wagon into one section and filled it with pineapples, and for a few weeks afterward, we engaged in a steady diet of them and traded the rest for other edible items. I have to admit that my passion for pineapple was diminished for a long time after consuming so many.

We spent some time on the north shore of Oahu. One morning after a lengthy surf session, we were starving, and Tom reminded me we had left our wallets behind, leaving us temporarily penniless. Stopping by the Haleiwa Sea Spree, a huge local fair, we learned of the popular ice cream eating contest and decided to enter to fill our stomachs and for the fun of it. There were a dozen of us on stage, and each was given ten rock-hard frozen pint Dixie cups to consume. There were some eating pros amongst the competition, so I knew creativity was a necessity. I opened all of my cups and put them in the sun as best I could to warm and soften their contents. The strategy worked, and I earned third place along with a full, though a bit unsettled, stomach.

Maui is a popular destination for celebrities, and we had a few wild encounters with some. After the restaurant closed each night, we would often go out for a beer at one of the local bars. Once we walked into one, and there was Tina Turner up on the small stage. She apparently was enjoying her time there and wanted to treat the other customers with a little show—quite a sight to see such vibrant energy close up!

Another evening, some surf buddies were sitting in a bar when Neil Young walked in. They struck up a conversation and convinced him to play a few songs. When they asked the owner, he did not know who Young was, and when the unkempt fellow was pointed out, he said it would be bad for business to put such a disheveled musician on stage. Not deterred, our buddies called a friend who ran another bar, who was excited about the opportunity. They talked Neil into relocating, and he used the piano there to share some great music.

In February, the Oakland Raiders won the Super Bowl, and many members of the team descended on Maui after their victory. Not surprisingly, it led to lots of excitement in town.

A number of the best surfers in the world visit Maui at some point in the winter. The veteran Owl Chapman used to sit way outside at

Honolua Bay on a huge, weathered board, seemingly far away from the best takeoff spot, but invariably, there would be a large set every now and then, and Owl would come riding through the scrambling crowd on a beaut!

Sometimes, the experience of engaging with the top surfers was challenging. South African champ Shaun Thomson was out with us at a nice break called Windmills one afternoon. He had a film crew with him who were trying to get some shots in the great waves, so he was extra aggressive with getting rides, causing us to be frustrated with our opportunities.

Obviously, surfing was our main focus, and there were so many memorable moments. One of my goals was to surf Honolua by myself, and one morning I paddled out before dawn and had just that for about an hour until others arrived. It was so special to be able to choose the best waves and to ride with a total focus on the path of their breaking without the tension of competing for them with all the other surfers. It was surfing at its best, but I slowly watched it slip away with the arrival of others in the lineup.

Living on a relatively small island allowed us to find waves virtually every day. If there were no swells near Honolua, we could usually drive to the east side and find waves at great breaks like Hookipa. Suffice it to say that I was thrilled with what nature provided during my stay there.

In March, we went to the north shore of Oahu and surfed the world-famous north shore breaks of Pipeline, Sunset, Velzyland, and Laniakea. I was at the top of my surfing game, but these spots stretched me. At Sunset, numerous times I thought I was set right for a take-off when the swell angle would shift slightly, a liquid monster would threaten to dump on me, and I was subsequently paddling for my life.

Pipeline was perfect the first day I rode it, big enough for memorable rides but small enough that I could handle its power. The water was so calm and clear that you could see the treacherous shallow reef clearly, even some of the caves that occasionally trap surfers, which provided an incentive not to fall.

The next day, a big swell arrived, and the number of people in the water dwindled noticeably. I just watched in awe at Pipeline as only a few brave souls were attempting to navigate the treacherous surf. I didn't have the right board or the courage to surf at Waimea Bay, but swam out into the channel to get a sense of the spot's power. It was a great reminder that although I was surfing well, there was a point where the size of the surf was beyond my capabilities.

My time in Hawaii was filled with thrilling, as well as frightening, moments that stretched my surfing capabilities, encounters with characters who broadened my life perspective, and lots of hilarious, unforgettable experiences. I left with an enhanced respect for the ocean and the surfers who ride big waves, a greater humility knowing my limitations, and an enhanced understanding of the diversity of people on our planet.

AUTHOR'S NOTES

When people ask for a recommendation on which of the eight major Hawaiian Islands to visit, I recommend Maui. Though relatively small, it has an incredible diversity of natural wonders. The towering Haleakala volcano, with its massive, scenic crater, is the first place the sun hits in the Pacific, and one can spend hours hiking there.

Another highlight is the road to the quaint town of Hana, where Charles Lindbergh was buried. While the road is only sixty miles long, it takes all day to get there due to the many twists and turns and fifty one-lane bridges. There are lots of wonderful beaches and swimming holes in the rivers on the scenic route, surrounded by lush jungle with a myriad of beautiful flowers.

There is a wet and dry side of the island that allows for diverse experiences in close proximity. The surrounding ocean provides great snorkeling and surfing. Unfortunately, the scenic, historic town of Lahaina was destroyed by fire in 2023 and is still recovering.

Hawaii is a very complex community. In a few short months, I saw numerous positives and negatives to living there. It is a tropical paradise, but people talk about "rock fever"—the sense that you can only drive an hour and then there is nothing but thousands of miles of ocean until the next bit of land. The social dynamic is very complex, balancing the friendliness of the people with the harm the native Hawaiians have endured from the many foreign influences, from the missionaries to the developers, from other cultures to the impact of tourism today.

Haleiwa ice cream eating contest

Tom and I modeling for the local tourist bureau in Lahaina

Beating the crowd by catching a smaller wave at Honolua Bay

COOKING WITH THE
KRISHNAS, AUSTRALIA | 1977

THE ONLY TIME MY FATHER EXPRESSED ANGUISH ABOUT my two-year, round-the-world travels was when he feared I was joining the Krishnas. A friend who had been passing through Coolangatta, the town where I was living on the Gold Coast of Australia, had snapped a photo of my Krishna-like haircut and mailed it to him. He was alarmed enough to send me a cautionary letter about joining the cult. Little did he know, the Krishnas of Coolangatta were very low on the danger scale for me in my worldly travels, but I was touched by his concern.

I had moved to this town primarily to surf the numerous world-class point breaks in the vicinity. In 1977, it was filled with many itinerant surfers and had evolved from a sleepy fishing town to a booming seaside resort. Around the time the photo of my Krishna haircut was taken, I had been living with an ex-boxer named Frankie and his delightful wife, Sylvia. Their home had been an ideal rental for my surfing purposes. It was right across the street from Kirra Point, one of the top breaks in Australia, and just down the road from the site of my construction job at a new apartment complex.

The area was quiet, rent was cheap, and they often included me for dinner. However, even with the low rent and free food, the living conditions were challenging.

Frankie's daily routine included nonstop consumption of beer, and he would often get verbally abusive with Sylvia in the evening. Sometimes when I returned from work, I would find her hiding under my bed, where she sought refuge. I did my best to comfort her, wondering if I should take steps such as confronting Frankie or even going to the police. However, since I was working illegally, without proper paperwork, I was nervous about getting involved with the law. Nevertheless, their relationship was extremely unsettling.

After a few weeks of living with this tension, I could not handle staying with this volatile couple any longer, and one evening, I left their home, searching for an alternative place to stay. As I strolled through town, I passed the window of my favorite pie shop and noticed a sign: "Free Health Food Feast and Mellow Spiritual Gathering." I was always looking for a free meal and a way to expand my social network, so I decided to see what this was all about.

I was excited when I realized that the event overlooked Point Danger and Duranbah, two of the many great surf breaks in Coolangatta. Indian music and Aussie voices emanated out of the restaurant, and I nervously opened the door, not knowing what to expect.

The room was reverberating; it hardly looked "mellow." People who were not eating were dancing and chanting; some wore colorful robes, and most of the men had extremely short haircuts. A friendly young woman introduced herself and explained the celebration. This group of Hare Krishna devotees had gathered for a festive chant and meal at their restaurant, The Bamboo Flute. They were advertising around town in the hopes of recruiting new devotees. I knew a little about the religion, and despite the cheerfulness of everyone in the room, I was aware of the controversy with the Krishnas concerning their cult-like activities and aggressive marketing in airports, as well as other venues in the United States.

Despite these concerns, I enjoyed the food and company that evening and got into a deep conversation with Maria, the friendly young woman at the door, who turned out to be the wife of the owner of the restaurant. After she explained their story, and I offered a summary of my work and travel, she shared that they needed some more cooks. I confirmed that I had worked in restaurants, and Maria offered me free room and board if I helped with dinners. This was perfect! If I cooked in the evening with the Krishnas at the "Flute," I could eat and sleep there for free, keep my construction job, and still have time to surf.

The next day, I shared a feeble excuse for needing to change my living quarters, moved out of Frankie and Sylvia's house near Kirra, and settled into my new home above the restaurant. My only hesitation was abandoning Sylvia, though I did check in with her intermittently during the rest of my stay in town.

The adjustment to rooming with the Krishnas began immediately. A few of them were staying on the same floor, and they explained to me that while living in their proximity, I needed to be sensitive to where they were spiritually (their higher chakra) and had to adhere to the tenets of the Krishna faith, for starters: no alcohol, no tobacco, and no playing of most music.

In addition, they clarified that I needed to follow the dietary restrictions for Krishna devotees in my cooking: no meat allowed in any dish, and when I shared my ingredients for a good vegetarian spaghetti, I was surprised to learn that I couldn't use mushrooms (considered a food of ignorance) or onions and garlic (foods of passion). At that point, I requested a Krishna cookbook and began to develop my adjusted repertoire.

Even with approved recipes, there were some additional adjustments I had to make as a cook. For example, when I prepared a dish, I was required to put one serving at the base of the altar to Krishna in the center of the kitchen. The premise was that Krishna would guide me to season the food appropriately before serving it to a customer. I did my best to sense his "guidance." I was only allowed to sample it myself afterwards and then alter the contents as necessary. There were times when I wanted to explain this practice to the unknowing customers, but that was not honoring their faith in Krishna.

During the first week, I squashed a cockroach that was skittering across the kitchen floor to the horror of my fellow chefs. I was kindly informed that Krishnas did not kill any animals, as every creature had a "spirit soul" that was not to be harmed. There was a place for cockroaches and all creatures in the kitchen, and I should let them be.

Despite the challenges of adjusting to the Krishna ways, I really respected and enjoyed my fellow workers and was fascinated by their way of living. They, in turn, accepted me, and friendships blossomed. They were intrigued by facets of my life, in particular my Quaker faith. Often, after our dinner responsibilities were completed, we would get into interesting discussions regarding religion and upbringing.

Slowly, a few of my new friends began asking questions regarding my openness to joining their group. One concrete step was a haircut. I had long, straggly hair and allowed one of them to give me a buzz, but I did not keep the one long strand, which they believed was needed to differentiate themselves from other Buddhist and Hindu sects, who also shaved their heads. The haircut was the only step I took in regard to following the tenets of the religion, and my Krishna friends accepted me even though I was not going to become a fellow devotee.

Living at the Flute worked well. I would get up early, go to the kitchen and make a huge smoothie with lots of fresh fruit, head to work at the construction site, go surfing in the afternoon, and cook dinner with the Krishnas at night. The only complicated day was Tuesday, when I had to make alternative plans for the evening. On that day, the Krishnas closed the restaurant for dinner and had a lengthy feast and resounding chant. The dinner began around five, and the rowdy chant of Hare Krishna, Hare Rama lasted until around ten. The length of the gathering was based on the belief that every time devotees uttered the phrase, they got closer to Krishna, some saying the words should be chanted at least 1000 times each day. I was amazed at their chanting stamina, but it was a bit much for me. I always made other plans on Tuesdays.

When my construction job ended, I started handling the Flute's new takeout window for lunches, where I had priceless conversations with customers, as I explained the Krishna diet and why a veggie burger and carob shake had to replace their request for a hamburger and a chocolate shake. We lost the business of a few questioning locals, but the Flute's takeout window did begin to build a following. My veggie burger became popular, but Mick, the owner, reminded me constantly, "Harvey, you did not make that burger; Krishna guided you to do so."

My discussions with my fellow restaurant workers revealed that while they considered themselves Krishna followers, they had left the main Australian group because of expectations that they felt were unreasonable. For example, each day they had been asked to go out on the streets of Melbourne and sell a certain number of Krishna record albums; the group looked down upon them if they were unsuccessful. Consequently, a number of the followers had moved to Coolangatta to start their own group that had practices they could accept as appropriate for a devotee.

I became particularly close to the restaurant owners, Mick and Maria, as well as Sachigra, the guitar maestro/spiritual leader of the group. I attended fascinating dinners in their homes, which included deep spiritual discussions, and they included me in their weekly hikes into the outback. Queensland's landscape changes quickly from the coastal woodlands to the arid landscape of the interior. Hiking on breathtaking trails with Mick and Sachigra allowed me to learn even more about the natural and social elements of Australia and the ways of Krishna followers. These walks also offered a break from the "rough and tumble" world of the Aussie surfers and construction workers who comprised the majority of my peer group.

In July, my girlfriend, Sherry, came to visit, and one last awkward Krishna moment transpired. When Mick heard she was coming, he informed me that one of the members who was living on the second floor with me was on such a high chakra (spiritual level) that he could not sleep near people who were intimate, unless it was for procreation. The consequences of that conversation were complex; say no more.

While I did not become a Krishna follower, the experience impacted my spiritual growth in a number of profound ways, most importantly, to try to understand the rationale for different faiths, not writing them off as fanatical, even if some of their practices and beliefs seemed strange. Living closely with people whose spiritual path was so different from my Quaker upbringing enhanced my appreciation for Friends' tenets but also allowed me to see how people benefited from different approaches to religion. The Krishna diet made a lot of sense; their life view was a healthy one for the most part, and the chant is embedded deeply in my memory.

Hara Krishna, Hare Krishna, Krishna Krishna, Hare Hare Hare Rama, Hare Rama, Rama Rama, Hare Hare

AUTHOR'S NOTES

Coolangatta is a beach town on the New South Wales/Queensland border, which is home to a number of the best point breaks in the country and consequently many surfers. The area has produced numerous world champions, and the competition for waves is intense. I did learn that Aussie surfers generally do not like to get up early, so often I went out at dawn to get some solitary waves. I was fortunate to be friends with a few of the locals, and they led me on some wild surf excursions up and down the East Coast of the country.

Although I had "employment prohibited" stamped in my passport, I landed a construction job in town, a needed step, as I was getting low on funds for the trip. I had to adjust to the Aussie work ethic and other idiosyncrasies of construction there. For example, my boss told me to be there at eight each morning, and I showed up punctually the first week, until I learned even he did not get there until 8:30. I also had to adjust to the different names for tools. The first day, my boss asked me to get a twister out of the ute; the translation is wrench out of the pickup. That work, coupled with free room and board at the Bamboo Flute, allowed me to save enough money to continue my travels with less financial anxiety.

The Hare Krishna, a branch of Hinduism that believes that Krishna is the supreme deity, has been around since the late 1400s. Devotees use the Bhagavad Gita as their religious text and follow most of the Hindu beliefs, such as reincarnation. Chanting, dancing, and meditation are key to this sect. As noted in the story, they have a pretty strict lifestyle.

In the 1960s, the Krishna movement gained popularity in the Western world but was simultaneously challenged as having some negative cultlike qualities. Numbers have dropped off in recent years, but the religion still has an international following.

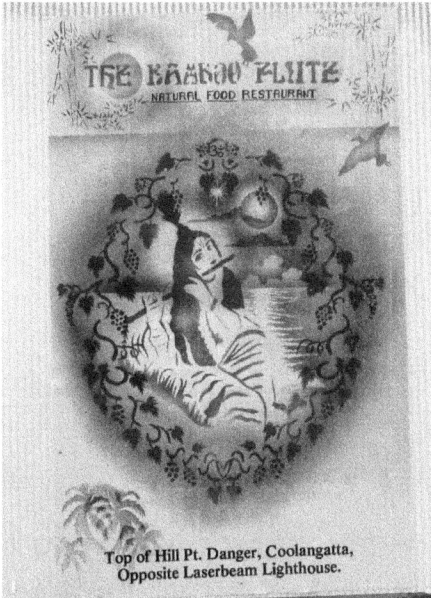

The Bamboo Flute flyer

Break for the cooks in front
of the Flute

Sachigra leading the Tuesday chant in full swing

FINDING ULUWATU AND A COKE, INDONESIA | 1977

THE SIDE OF THE ROAD WAS CROWDED WITH LOCALS, carrying babies, bundles of supplies, chickens, cats, and a myriad of other household items. We were all getting into the bemo, a glorified pickup truck with an enclosed back, the standard public transportation on Bali. I found a place to wedge my surfboard, eager to get to Ulu, the epic stories about this surf spot fueling my excitement.

Once in the bemo, the wooden seats were uncomfortable, the speed was slow, the air was hot and smoky, but we seemed to be headed out of town in the right direction. The local passengers exchanged glances and smiles. I was curious about their stories, and sure, they were wondering about mine. After a few stops with locals hopping on and off, the driver came to the back and announced, "Uluwatu!"

"Here?" I muttered, trying to show a sense of confidence as I looked with disbelief at the dirt path with no visible signs of humanity nearby. This could *not* be the way to one of the world's most famous surf breaks. The driver nodded and winked sheepishly, affirming the location and acknowledging my trepidation.

Sherry and I squirmed and twisted our way through our fellow travelers to the back of the jammed truck and climbed down into the desert-like landscape. My unsettled girlfriend and I stared at the packed-down footpath leading to a parched field with no hint of the classic lefthander, a wave, which, as viewed from the beach, breaks from left to right. How could this trail lead to one of the greatest surf breaks in the world?

Nevertheless, we began our hike down the trail. Pencil cacti and Burmese fishtail palm dotted the arid landscape, a real contrast to the lush jungle that covers most of Bali. The lightening-fast chirping geckos and silent skinks on this path could have kept me captivated for hours—if it were not for one thing: my snake phobia.

Bali is known for its venomous snakes. In some public toilets, there are signs warning occupants to look for cobras before doing their business. These signs heightened my sensitivity to snakes on the path to Uluwatu. While I had not yet seen any of these creatures, I definitely spotted holes with unseen occupants—potential homes amongst the rocks for my slithery nemeses.

Walking on the dusty trail for over thirty minutes, I began to wonder if we had been misled by the bemo driver. Then, finally, I heard the familiar sound of waves crashing on a reef and felt the freshness of an ocean breeze overtake the hot, arid air. As is customary when reaching a new, challenging break, my heart rate increased, and a small knot began to grow in my stomach.

Jitters are a part of the surf experience. Although I felt increasingly confident from previously surfing El Salvador's La Libertad, Maui's Honolua Bay, Oahu's North Shore Pipeline and Sunset Beach, New Zealand's Raglan Point, and most recently Bali's Kuta Reef, like many experienced surfers, I face the heebie-jeebies when approaching beaches with some of the most daunting waves in the world.

Unlike other portions of the trip, I had not spoken with many people who had surfed Ulu, so when Sherry and I came over a rise to finally see the powerful waves marching to shore, I was in awe of the towering cliffs but shocked that I did not see a single surfer. Nobody was there, nobody to show me how to get down the cliffs into the water, nobody to tell me how to navigate the shallow reef through the powerful surf, and nobody to point out the best spot to catch these pounding waves. Although I had heard Uluwatu frequently referenced, here I was with no one to look to for guidance. Perhaps this absence of surfers was because Uluwatu had only been "discovered" as a surfing destination a few years earlier, after being featured in a movie and an article in Surfer Magazine.

The absence of other surfers was a tough realization, in part because I was still recovering from a head wound I'd received two days earlier, learning the hard way about the power of the waves at Kuta Beach. Storms forming thousands of miles away in Antarctica generate huge swells, and the first reefs they encounter are on the southern shores of Bali. But even with a significant gash in my forehead, there was no way I was going to let anyone on this island stitch me up, after recently witnessing the tragedy of a French acquaintance.

Artemis had been riding his motorcycle to a remote break when a bump from a pothole sent him to the hospital with a severely broken leg. Since it needed to be set, he was given some Indonesian anesthesia that successfully knocked him out. When he awoke, he looked down to examine the break, only to discover that the bottom half of his leg was gone. The doctors explained they were worried about infection, so removing a portion of the limb was the best option, the catch being that they cut off his leg without getting his take on the consequences. Artemis was taken to a plane to return to France in a straitjacket. After witnessing this nightmare, I preferred a permanent scar on my forehead to visiting the local hospital. Accidents and injuries do not stop the passionate waverider, but they are part of the reason why most experienced surfers have the jitters when approaching a new break of the caliber and remoteness of Uluwatu.

So here I was, gazing at these waves crashing on the reef, doubting my ability to even get out to them if it was going to be a solitary venture. Good surfers always size up a break before entering it, and there is an advantage in watching other riders in the water to learn from their successes and mistakes. I was not afforded this benefit. The knot in my stomach got tighter, and my heart rate was on the upswing when I heard the familiar Australian cracks behind us on the path.

"Eh, Jack, Good on ya!"

"Yeah, you little ripper!"

As I turned to witness the commotion, along came three surfers and a film crew. In classic Aussie style, they explained they were making a movie and invited me to join them to "get some yank footage in the flick." With my fifteen years of surfing experience, I had become pretty adept at sizing up talent before entering the water, and it was obvious to me that these were some studs from "down under." It turned out that the quietest one, named Terry, was one of the top professionals in the world.

The frenzy began, unpacking of the filming devices, waxing of boards, slapping on a little lotion, all the while immersed in the banter that typically comes with a surf session. I entered into the buzz, but my stomach continued to knot. Rick, the most outspoken of the bunch, led us to a break in the cliff edge, and we began the steep descent to a cave.

The path itself was not that challenging, though one was constantly watching for loose rocks, and there was a need for handholds in spots. The Aussie banter died down until we got to the bottom and entered a small cave. The view of the waves through the opening took on a whole different perspective. Instead of looking down at the swells from a distance, you were staring at the six-to-eight-foot walls crashing over the shallow reef, only twenty yards from the cliffs, their frothy remnants covering the small bit of sand and rushing around our legs. The roar of the waves echoing in the cave made communicating with words challenging. The collective adrenaline amongst us was on the upswing.

Just as we slipped on our leashes and prepared to enter the water, the jokester, Rick, gleefully warned us to watch out for the sea snakes on this side of the reef. He said they were called "1, 2, 3's"; you might survive the first two bites, but the third was deadly. Given my phobia of snakes, this was almost enough to keep me out of the ocean.

I carefully navigated the water near shore, watching nervously for the jagged, dangerous coral heads and any slithering friends. After a few yards of walking through the shallow water, I realized there was too much coral to avoid, so I followed the lead of my Aussie mates, hopped on my board, and began the paddle into the awaiting tumultuous white water, often called "nature's washing machine."

I intuitively knew when to paddle hard, when to wait for the power of the ocean to subside, and what was the best angle to approach the massive swell. I fell behind the others in this endeavor, took some beatings that resulted in lost breath and ground, but eventually saw a treasured lull and sprinted for open water. One of the many great feelings in surfing is that moment of relief when you realize you have made it past the break and can sit up on your board, rest for a moment, and survey the waves from a place of relative tranquility.

Once we all made it to this safety zone, the four of us were spread out, but soon we began to converge while constantly eyeing the open ocean for the larger sets that broke further out. Having already managed plenty of physical and mental challenges, now was the most significant one: dropping into one of these steep monsters and riding it to safety.

It wasn't long before I was the only one who had not caught a wave. I paddled into one but hesitated when I looked down its steep face. Then, it was time; I knew it was just a question of confidence. The next set provided me with an opportunity to catch one of the "easier" waves, and I stroked into it, finding the drop not as lethal as it looked.

The adrenaline and focus of the ride took over, sizing up short-term maneuvers while keeping an eye down the wall for upcoming decisions. The wave was more forgiving and predictable than I had anticipated. Eventually, when I saw the looming coral heads and a section that offered a marginal escape, I made a quick exit over the top of the wave, flopped into the warm water, and paused for a moment, enjoying that sense of exhilaration and satisfaction of a great ride. Yet the interlude was short-lived, as I eyed a set coming in and realized I needed to move seaward quickly to avoid the wrath of these powerful swells.

I was now paddling with a renewed sense of confidence, reinforced by a smile and thumbs up from one of my newfound friends. Sizing up which ensuing wave to take got easier and easier with the increased comfort from each ride.

How many times in your life does adversity strike just when you let your guard down? As I paddled back to the lineup, I heard a shriek from Rick and saw his look of fear and shock. I realized his shriek said "shark," and when I followed his pointing hand, there were three gigantic sharklike shadows beneath the clear water. Our reactions were identical: catch the nearest wave, don't even try to surf it, but simply ride it to the cave as quickly as possible. Our focus shifted from riding great waves to a rapid exit. There was no communication amongst any of us until our feet hit the sand of the cave, and even then, we just gazed at each other, silently communicating, "Did you see those monsters?"

Australians are more accustomed to seeing sharks than Americans, but this was different. There was no space for us in the water with those creatures. After a few minutes of gathering our composure, we began the hike back up the trail. When we reached the top, the scene went from being terrifying to perplexing. The edge of the cliff was filled with Balinese, throwing offerings of flowers, food, and other items into the sea. Uluwatu has a spiritual significance, but why were there so many people leaving such an abundance of gifts today?

I learned shortly from one of the Balinese who spoke English that this was a day to commemorate their struggle against the Japanese rule during World War II. According to the locals, a few Balinese had jumped to their death off these very cliffs to avoid living under the Japanese. On this day, the Balinese commemorate the resistance by throwing offerings over the edge to the evil spirits, claiming there are always demons in the water on the anniversary. The Balinese are known for their devotion to the world of spirits. On this day, it manifested itself in a strange but beautiful manner. After a few minutes of fascination, we all felt as if today this place was for the Balinese, not the intruding surfers, and so we began to quietly pack up our gear and exit the cliff area.

The walk back took on a solemn air; we had all just been through two hours of thrills, scares, and finally the witnessing of a tradition that was beyond our Western understanding. Why would a person sacrifice his life to protest the injustice of the occupation?

We were walking against the human traffic on their way down the path heading to the cliff edge, men and women dressed in colorful outfits carrying offerings. I was fascinated by their clothing and what they were carrying, but tried to avoid staring out of respect for the purpose of their pilgrimage. The steady stream increased in numbers as we approached the road, and once we came to the macadam, we were astonished to see the crowds making their way to the water.

I had been so enthralled with the experience for the past hour that I was distracted from my own condition. Yet, once we arrived at the road, I realized that the combination of the crowds, the intensity of the surfing, and the omnipresent heat had caught up with me. I felt lightheaded and a bit nauseous.

When we had arrived earlier in the morning, I hadn't noticed the food stand on the other side of the road, at the entrance to the path. Now it was bustling with business, mostly feeding pilgrims and a few surfers who had just arrived and learned that it was not a good day to be in the water here.

I sat under a frangipani tree to steady myself when Sherry handed me a Coke. The familiar taste and texture of the soda soothed my nauseous stomach, and the juxtaposition of enjoying a lukewarm Coke, after everything we had experienced on this day, seemed ironic, and made for a deeper respect for the Balinese and a cherished memory.

AUTHOR'S NOTES

This experience happened in 1977. When I returned to Bali in 2014, there was a good road to the cliffs and a fancy resort with an infinity pool perched by its edge. The path down to the cave is cluttered with restaurants as well as souvenir and surf shops tucked into little perches in the cliffs. It is said that Uluwatu and the surrounding surf breaks generate $35 million a year in tourist dollars, more than any other surfing destination in the world. However, the waves and the reef remain the same, a challenge to any surfer. Do the sharks still show up on that special day of commemoration? I didn't ask.

As noted in the story, Uluwatu is a surf break on the coast of Bali, which is one of the 13,000 islands that comprise Indonesia, the largest Muslim country in the world. Its draw was the fantastic surf, but Bali, more than any other place I visited, was so much more than a location to ride great waves.

Known for its beautiful art, gamelan music, and colorful, exotic festivals, a traveler never ceases to be enchanted by the people and natural beauty. As an itinerant surfer, I would have to rest my body periodically from the physical toll of riding waves, which allowed me to have time to explore this fascinating island. High points included hikes through the verdant rice paddies and jungle filled with monkeys and other exotic animals, up the slopes of volcanoes, and into the fascinating villages.

I stayed near Kuta Beach during most of my time there and could walk out at night and witness cock fights, beautiful dancers, and many other sights and sounds unique to the island. I enjoyed the spicy food, though I did have a bout of "Bali belly," which is quite unpleasant but a common challenge for visitors. Thankfully, I never encountered a snake!

The religion of Bali is a fascinating one, a combination of Hinduism, Buddhism, and ancient local beliefs as seen in the art, festivals, temples, and many other facets of the society.

With all these wonderful attributes, it is no surprise that Bali has become a very popular destination for international travel, with all the obvious positive and negative consequences.

View of the waves from the cave

Connection of surfers and worshippers

Arrival of the film crew

The break as viewed from the cliffs

BEYOND EXPLANATION,

MALAYSIA | 1977

═══════════

I CANNOT SCIENTIFICALLY OR LOGICALLY EXPLAIN AN event that I witnessed in Malaysia. It is a story that is difficult for me to tell and one that I have rarely shared.

I first met Surrander at a park in the seaside town of Penang. In my travels, I love to meet locals, and since there were no surfers nearby with whom to connect, I worked my way into a friendly game of soccer. As we finished, Surrander struck up a conversation with me. He skipped the superficial questions that are often part of an initial chat with someone and went right to thoughtful issues involving my observations of Penang and how it differed from my own community. Towards the end of our deeply introspective dialogue, he invited me to stay with his family. Intrigued by his thoughtfulness and curiosity, I said yes with little hesitation.

After gathering my belongings from the hostel, we were off to Surrander's home. On the way, he proudly described his family of four: his Sikh father, Muslim mother, and "Western" brother, Ben. Surrander warned me that despite everyone getting along, there were four strong, diverse characters living under one roof.

It is amazing how brothers who come from the same parents and are raised in a shared environment can be so different. Ben was outgoing, athletic, and comfortable in any social situation. Surrander was thoughtful, quiet, and hesitant to engage with most people. Ben was muscular and stocky; Surrander was tall and gaunt. Their parents shared many of the typical gender stereotypes: dad, as the boss of the house, mom, the pleaser/worker bee, but both were extremely inquisitive and strong-minded.

This eclectic family welcomed me into their home. They invited me on cultural excursions and treated me to numerous delectable meals during my week-long stay. While enjoying elaborate, lengthy dinners, we had deep conversations about life, making each day robust, intense, and thought-provoking. Throughout my visit, I appreciated the welcoming comfort of such a dynamic family.

I met Surrander first, but I spent most of my time with Ben. Though Surrander was with us only periodically, when he did join us, there was always a profundity to the experience. For example, he was curious about my fears. He said that while he was impressed with my stories of riding big waves, there must be some facets of nature that I found intimidating. When I mentioned my snake phobia, he quickly responded with a plan for a field trip he thought might help me, though he thought it was not wise to share details. I was curious about his plans, but honored his request of making them a surprise and did not prod him for more specifics.

On the morning of the adventure, Surrander showed an energy I had not seen before. As I ate breakfast, he was already packing a lunch and advising me about what to wear, all the while keeping our destination a secret. There was a brisk pace to all that he did, and we were soon off through the crowded side streets of Penang, Surrander, the organized, deliberate leader with me, as the curious follower. As we rounded one particular corner, he paused and pointed to a tiny, ornate temple in the middle of the busy city block. While it was no larger than its neighboring restaurants and stores, the building looked out of place with its golden statues and colorful scenes of deities, dragon-like figures, and snakes. The wide entrance was highlighted by large white pillars with graphic reliefs of other-worldly creatures engaged in a variety of activities.

Surrander's tone changed a bit as he shared that it was time to reveal our destination: a Buddhist Snake Temple. While the outside of the building gave no hint of its unique purpose, the interior was filled with altars and statues wrapped in various manners by live snakes, some of which were allegedly lethal pit vipers. It was built in the 1800s to honor a tenth-century Buddhist monk who was known for taking care of the sick and giving shelter to snakes. He explained it was safe to go inside during the day because there was incense burning, which made the snakes sleepy. Visitors would leave offer-ings of mice and other animals, and at night, when the smoke died down, the snakes would come to life and partake in the offerings. This description seemed somewhat unbelievable but sparked my curiosity.

Given my deep-rooted fear of snakes, I was obviously hesitant about entering the temple, but fear of disappointing Surrander gave me little choice. As I gingerly followed him through the front door, one of the hosting monks smiled at me and pointed above my head. When I looked up, there was a snake lounging on a rafter just above me. I worked to calmly move past the opening, wondering how he had sensed my discomfort.

With that unsettling entrance, I wandered slowly through the ornate rooms. Comforted by the alleged impact of the incense, I passed the Dragon Eye Wells and two giant brass bells, but I couldn't say that I ever truly relaxed as I walked around the temple. I was amazed at the diversity of the altars and the various ways the snakes were draped around them, though with each step, I was alert to not get too close or be surprised by the serpents' proximity. Surrander's insights enhanced the experience, though he stretched my appear-ance of calm when he made the suggestion that he take a picture of me with these creatures. I gave him my camera and moved closer to one of the snake-filled altars. He smiled as he said I should get a little closer for a good picture. To this day, the photograph documents my unsettled nerves. I never really relaxed until we exited the temple.

As we headed home, Surrander shared his observations of my level of comfort in the temple and was curious if the experience in any way made me more at ease with the source of my phobia. He was such an earnest soul that while I did not want to hurt his feelings, I felt compelled to be truthful. I shared that the experience was fascinating, but I am afraid I could not relax while in the company of these slithery creatures. However, I expressed my gratitude for all he did to make the day special, and maybe in the long run it might have an impact on my phobia. Nobody else in my life had ever gone to such an extent to try to lessen my fears.

Despite this profound experience with Surrander, most of my engagement throughout the week was with Ben and his girlfriend. Ben was so excited to spend time with, as he said, "a true, red-blooded American." He knew so much about our country and hoped to visit someday. He was eager to show off his American friend to every contact in Penang, so our daily activities were quite extensive.

The soccer field was the one source of familiarity amongst the exotic locales we visited. Even though I was one of the worst players on the pitch, Ben was very positive about my athletic prowess, and the experience allowed me to meet a number of his friends and observe our different worlds in a unique way. For example, it was not unusual for practices to be interrupted by a herd of oxen traipsing across the field, often leaving presents on the grass.

One day during a scrimmage, the normally easygoing players engaged in a vicious fistfight over a questionable play. The brawl ended as quickly as it started, and the game resumed as if nothing had happened, despite the bruises and blood on the players. I had played soccer for a number of years, but these unique moments allowed a usually familiar game to be somewhat perplexing to me. However, I relished this opportunity to connect with this facet of

Malaysian life, appreciating the differences from my usual soccer experience.

The generosity of the family was so profound during my time with them that I offered to prepare an American dinner for our last meal together. We had a riotous shopping spree, the challenge being to find authentic American ingredients in the Malay markets. The menu included spaghetti, garlic bread, and salad. Instead, we ended up with hot dogs and baked beans along with the planned cake and ice cream for dessert, as we had to go with what was available at the local stores.

While I was preparing the American feast as creatively as I could, Ben took me aside to share that Surrander had a special gift for me after dinner, but we would have to wait until his parents were in bed. I was so focused on my cooking challenges that I never gave much thought to his words or to the question of why we had to wait for the parents to go upstairs.

Though some people might question the authenticity of this "American" meal, the family accepted it with interest. There was the usual upbeat spirit at the table, and I think they were appreciative of my intentions and effort, even if the final product was lackluster.

Once the kitchen was in some semblance of order and their parents had gone to bed, Ben called me into the living room, saying it was time for the "gift." I noticed a slight change in Surrander's demeanor, but nothing could have possibly prepared me for what happened next.

Ben, his girlfriend, and I were sitting quietly on the rug when Surrander entered and carefully set down a small bowl of burning embers in the center of the room. Focusing on the dish and not on us, he calmly began a series of chants along with movements that reminded me of Tai Chi. We observed Surrander with reverence, although I was unclear as to what was happening and was not sure how to react.

As he focused on the smoldering embers in the bowl, a subtle change came over him. Eventually, he lifted his head, looked into my eyes with an expression that was unrecognizable, and after a brief greeting began to talk about me, noting facets of my being that I had not shared with him, everything from some of my anxieties to references to experiences in my upbringing. As I listened, my mind was racing in a confused state, trying simultaneously to absorb what he was saying, while thinking how he knew so much about me.

Surrander was incredibly insightful, but some of the comments required more than simply observing and getting to know me. For example, he talked of my love of teaching, but noted that I was usually nervous before each class. This perception was absolutely accurate, but I could not remember ever discussing it with him. To add to my unease, his voice was husky and thick, not the voice of Surrander for which I was accustomed.

I listened, so captivated that I did not notice him removing a piece of ornate thread from his pocket and moving it slowly over the embers. He continued speaking; his insights into my being continued to be penetrating and unnerving. As he mentioned my upcoming departure to Thailand, he held up the thread and tied it to my finger, saying it would bring me good luck if I prayed daily to Buddha. It was then that I noticed his hands. As he tied the string around my finger, they were not those of a young man. His wrinkled fingers shook as he tied the knot.

With the process complete, he stared into my eyes and asked whether or not I wanted to know what to expect in the coming months. Awestruck and shaken by the previous dialogue, I nervously said that while I was curious, I liked the idea of not knowing what was next for me. I was simply too unnerved by what had transpired in the last few minutes that I feared what he might say. With a serene look, he returned to the movements that began his transition. After a few minutes, I felt he was, once again, Surrander. He stood up and exited the room without looking at us.

Dumbfounded, I looked to Ben for an explanation. He shared that Surrander had spent a great deal of time at a local Buddhist

monastery, and recently several priests had been teaching him complex practices, one of which involved changing spirits with another
person. The priests had chosen Surrrander because they felt they
could trust him with such powers. Ben explained to me that the
person who was engaging with me this evening was not Surrander
but an elderly priest with whom Surrander had temporarily switched
"personas." I later learned that this process essentially involves
exchanging consciousness or inhabiting another's body. This was
not the first time Ben had witnessed his brother's transition. While
he was excited for Surrander, Ben worried that the experience was
taking a toll on him, both physically and mentally. The serious, concerned tone of his responses to my questions revealed a side of Ben
I had not seen all week.

Simultaneously overwhelmed and curious, I listened to Ben's explanation. It defied Western logic. Not knowing what to do next, I suggested that we have dessert. The juxtaposition of eating ice cream and
cake after such a profound experience added to the intensity and irony
of the evening. Eventually, Surrander joined us. I thanked him for his
"gift," but we had little interaction. It is difficult to capture the multitude of emotions that ran through me. I was awestruck and moved,
full of wonder and confusion. Clearly, Surrander wanted to help me.
I knew it was a gesture of kindness, so I thanked him, but I know he
sensed my unease, as I had difficulty knowing what else to say.

That night, I did not sleep very much, wondering whether or
not Surrander's transition was a trick, wondering whether or not I
should have allowed him to tell me my future, and wondering what
lay ahead for me in my travels in Asia.

The next morning, my last one with Surrander's family, his
mother prepared a glorious meal. I expressed gratitude for all the
family had done for me. I thanked Ben as well as Surrander for showing me Penang, and expressed appreciation for our final evening
together, explaining how the experience had stretched me. I offered
sincere thankfulness and respect for his "gift," though my uneasiness

with it remained deep in my thoughts. His parents were with us, so I did my best to not alert them as to what had happened after they went to bed and my resulting angst from the experience.

Ben took me to the train station, where I headed north to Thailand. As is usual for Asia, the cars were packed. I finally found a seat next to a young French woman, who was eager to engage in conversation. She was new to Asia and wanted to tap me for any wisdom. When she asked about Penang, I spoke at length about the family who took me in, my experience at the Buddhist Snake Temple, and what I learned about playing soccer in Malaysia. I did not share the experience of my final night with Surrander. I was not ready to describe what had happened to anyone and wondered if I ever could.

To this day, I rarely tell this story, as it unsettles people. The experience left me with many questions: what is the scope of human potential, what is the connection between the physical and spiritual worlds, to name a few, but the sincerity of Surrander's generosity and the novelty of the experience redefined for me the idea of a gift. I often pause when someone says they have something for me, wondering if Surrander's will ever be matched.

AUTHOR'S NOTES

The state of Penang is located on the Northwest coast of Malaysia. Formerly a British colony, it is now a thriving, cosmopolitan community that attracts international tourists and economic development. My brief stay with a local family allowed me to see many of the most beautiful parts of the city and gain fascinating insights into the culture, the final evening being the most profound one.

As described in the story, I witnessed a personal transformation beyond my comprehension on the last night. Surrander was closely connected with the local Buddhist community, which is known for complex spiritual experiences. Abhijina is the term for certain powers and knowledge which go beyond what is explainable to most humans. Some Buddhists believe they can consult with mediums who are capable of telepathy, telekinesis, and other supernatural powers. Naturally, some of these are verifiable, while others are not. I was so overwhelmed by my experience that I am challenged to explain it. What I do know is there was something that evening which showed me a power that seemed to be beyond any I have ever witnessed.

While Buddhists are best known for these powers, Hindus and other Asian religions have similar qualities. I learned of Himalayan monks who were trained to control their body temperature, with the final test being drying a soaked sheet in freezing temperatures with only their body heat. Hiking through the mountain communities in Nepal, one intermittently connects with such groups who are engaging in similar fascinating practices.

Simply put, there is a segment of the population who have devoted themselves to developing skills that allow them to experience life in a way that is beyond the understood realities of most of humanity. I feel fortunate that, in a small way, I was able to experience this unique facet of society.

Connecting with the snakes

The Snake Temple

The soccer team cooling off; Surrander is in the back row, second from the right

A BURMESE MARRIAGE,

MYANMAR | 1977

I STARED ONE MORE TIME AT THE ITEMS I WAS ABOUT to purchase: two cartons of 555 cigarettes and a fifth of Johnny Walker Black Label Scotch. Not being a smoker or a partaker of whisky, and a bit of a cheapskate, the idea of "buying" these items seemed absurd. However, I had been told that their resale value outside the airport in Rangoon would cover my expenses for one week in Burma, the amount of time the government allotted foreign travelers to remain in the country in 1977.

The customers behind me in the duty-free shop in the Bangkok airport were losing their patience, so I nervously completed the transaction and exited with my more confident travel partners. The three of us had connected in the much safer country of Singapore a few weeks earlier. Traveling through Southeast Asia, one would intermittently spot a Westerner with a backpack and engage in conversation. Sometimes there would be a mutual connection, plans would be altered, and a group formed. Such was the experience with the three of us, the common thread being the desire to visit Burma with a few other stops along the way. Why Burma? We had learned of its current unique circumstances of isolation and fascinating history, and were intrigued, even more so because many travelers said to avoid it for safety reasons in addition to the many hurdles of visitation. That piqued our interest all the more!

How did we form this trio, me, being the American surfer who combined calm with an urge to take risks, Rozita, a smart, well-travelled Australian who was part Italian, Moroccan, and Portuguese and could pass as a local anywhere, and Julie, the hilarious Aussie who added the fun factor to every experience? We quickly found that traveling as a trio enhanced our experience in a myriad of ways, and despite our differences, we really enjoyed each other's company and unique qualities.

As we moved up the Malay Peninsula, we would share adventures, split up when our goals differed, and always have a plan to reconnect at a later date. Highlights included a trek through the Golden Triangle, an exotic region in northern Thailand, known for its drug trafficking and intriguing hill tribes. We began our trip in a treacherously narrow motorized canoe on a tributary of the Mekong and then departed to hike a trail through the jungle amongst some fascinating remote villages, filled with opium dens and other unique structures. Life in these communities included practices unseen in the rest of the country, such as bathing in dust rather than water and using only one hut, which was perched above the others in the village, to procreate.

There were a few nervous moments, such as when we encountered a group of Thai adolescents armed with U.S. automatic weapons along a remote section of the trail. We gave a perfunctory smile and nod as they passed, while our nerves surged, wondering about the need for those weapons in the area, and knowing that the recent end to the Vietnam War had left many unexplained wounds in this society. The otherworldliness of these remote villages revealed the diversity of Asian cultures. Experiences such as this one enhanced my willingness to engage in unclear or nerve-racking situations, and our entrance into Burma would most likely be another one.

The first day in the country proved to be just that. We had been told that the resale value of the cigarettes and whisky outside the airport in Rangoon would pay for the short time the Burmese government allotted foreign travelers entering the country in 1977. It proved to be true.

When we walked out of the Rangoon airport, we were hounded by buyers, teenagers yelling, "555 carton?, bottle Johnny Walker Black?" Within minutes, we finalized the sale of our goods and had enough Burmese currency for a week's visit.

Rozita smiled with an "I told you so" look, "Harvey, now do you trust me?"

I replied, "Of course, I trust you. I just didn't want to get stuck with thirty dollars of cigs and whisky when I don't enjoy either."

This was followed by a friendly lecture. "Sometimes you've gotta take a chance and open your wallet, Harvey. You're the one who convinced me to go hiking in the Golden Triangle, and you're worried about wasting a few bucks?" I knew she was right. I always took risks, except when it came to spending a few more dollars.

I remember Julie chiming in, "Hey, you two, we only have a week in Burma; are we gonna spend it arguing in this parking lot?" Impulsive Julie was right; the three of us had taken this detour in our Asian travels to explore a very complex country. Burma was doing its best to keep the trappings of Western culture out of its national ethos by limiting visitors' length of stay and requiring entrances and exits only by plane. We had been told to be ready for a society that had not changed much since the forties and was taking steps to keep it that way.

The ride into Rangoon from the airport confirmed what we had been told. We were transported in old army jeeps on bumpy, unpaved roads and noticed that most cars were from the 1940s. There were very few signs of the current 1970s Asia. It felt as if we had stepped back thirty years.

Our driver left us off near the Shwedagon Pagoda, one of the most magnificent structures in Asia. Perched on a hill, the 367-foot-tall structure is covered in gold, diamonds, and other jewels, and allegedly contains relics of the Buddha, including eight hairs from his head. We were impressed with the structure and the surrounding scene: monks performing various rituals and signs of the goodness of humanity on display in various modes, families enjoying the sights, vendors hawking exotic food, musicians sharing their talents, all with this amazing pagoda as a backdrop.

It was getting late in the afternoon, and time to get organized. As we left the area surrounding the pagoda, the contrasting realities of Burma began to surface, extreme poverty reflected in the lack of many commercial establishments and hordes of visibly hungry people, coupled with a strong police and military presence. These were just some of the signs of the challenges facing the citizens of this country.

We had been told that the only safe place to stay in Rangoon was the YMCA. Even by Asian standards, it was barely adequate. There were two large dusty rooms containing cots filled with a variety of eccentric characters, and communal bathrooms that were so dirty and with such foul odors that they necessitated only brief visits. It seemed relatively safe, but the omnipresent noise and stench made the prospect of a good night's sleep very unlikely.

Seeing little alternative, we checked in and hoped to at least find a decent place to have dinner. One of Rozita's gifts was her sense for finding restaurants that prepared food that was tasty and safe. Rangoon tested her ability, but she found an open-air, relatively clean eatery nearby. As we were finishing our meal, the conversation turned to what lay ahead for us.

Julie began, "I hope there's more to this country than Rangoon. Harvey, let's keep the riskiness of our adventure to a minimum!"

I agreed, "Tonight's accommodation might provide enough excitement for me."

Experienced Rozita chimed in. She had done her usual networking and shared that heading north by train, where it was allegedly cleaner, we'd have a more picturesque and culturally rich adventure, with the benefit of a cooler climate. Out of nowhere, a young man nearby grinned and said in perfect English, "That is a good idea!"

We all turned to find a handsome young Burmese fellow who introduced himself as Ricky. He pulled up a chair and, surprisingly, began conversing about his country in decent English. His enthusiasm for life and reflections on Burma were enticing, and he quickly offered to be our tour guide. Excited about his presence but leery of the pitfalls of such a connection, we tentatively agreed to meet him the next day at the Rangoon train station, without a promise of any compensation for his services.

The night's rest at the YMCA proved to be about as good as we expected: snoring, people talking in their sleep, various forms of smoke billowing above our cots, bathroom noises along with the constant commotion on the streets, all adding up to a weary trio in the morning. We exited the Y quickly and headed off to meet Ricky, excited for the next adventure and hoping for an improvement in our accommodations.

The train station was classic Asia, hot, crowded, chaotic, with no written or spoken signs of English and overwhelming even for us seasoned travelers. We welcomed Ricky's assistance. He helped us purchase the right ticket and find the appropriate track, so we agreed to have him join us. Stepping onto the railroad car, we were about to engage in one more eye-opening facet of life here. The slow-moving, noisy, smoky, overcrowded train was a clear example of Burma not budging from the forties. The wooden seats and floors were covered in reddish, foul-smelling betel nut residue, the stimulant of choice for the Burmese, much more omnipresent than chewing tobacco. Some passengers were carrying chickens, plants, a variety of food, blankets, and other household items. Some were asleep in the luggage racks above the open windows, which added to our wonderment at this overwhelming scene.

Ricky talked the entire time, sharing history, geography, and various social sciences in his description of the land and its populace, a welcome distraction from the train's sights and smells. However, whenever government agents came through the car to check everyone's documents, at Ricky's request, we had to awkwardly hide him under our seats. There was definitely more to his story, but we hesitated to push him for more personal details at this point in the trip, since his presence seemed more an advantage than a liability.

Our first destination was Mandalay, the capital of central Burma. Located on the banks of the Irrawaddy River, it is known for its beautiful palace and pagodas. We fell into a good tourist rhythm, with Ricky as our guide, enjoying the security of his company and traversing a manageable city that did not exhibit Rangoon's poverty and political complexities. The impressive historic structures gave us hints of the former glory of this society that contrasted with the impoverished life of its current inhabitants. We were also pleased to find a relatively clean, quiet hotel, though Ricky could not stay with us for some legal reason. However, he found lodging in a nearby Buddhist temple. This twist, coupled with having to hide him on the train, enhanced my concern regarding his circumstances, though Julie kept saying that I was overreacting and to stop worrying.

After a good day of exploration, we settled into a wonderful evening meal that ended with a bombshell; Ricky and Julie announced that they were going to get married, not for the conventional reasons but to get him out of the country. They enthusiastically shared that all that was necessary was a visit to the Australian embassy, with Julie showing she had at least $1000 to her name. I was speechless.

When did they have time to come up with this radical idea? Did Julie really know what she was getting into? She and Ricky agreed nonchalantly that once they got out of the country, they would go their separate ways.

In shock, Rozita and I simply nodded and kept a poker face, not showing our concerns about Julie's decision until we separated and returned to our respective rooms for the evening. Julie was an adventurous young woman, but her impulsivity with this path was scary to us both. We had not known her long enough to play the big brother/

sister role and warn her of our worries, but we did not feel right letting her proceed with this crazy plan.

The next morning we felt Julie must have sensed our concern, as when Rozita and I went to meet them downstairs at the hotel, there was a short note sharing that Julie and Ricky had taken an early train to Rangoon to escape from some police issues that I did not understand and to begin the marriage process, as there were only four days left on her one-week visa. Reservations regarding their relationship continued to mount, but we decided to continue with our original plans, sensing we would not be successful in altering Julie's matrimonial path. That being said, we both felt torn between our desire to see more of this intriguing country and still be responsible travel companions for Julie, our acquaintance of just a few weeks.

Nonetheless, Rozita and I traveled on to Maymyo, a fascinating small town, formerly a British Hill Station and summer capital during the colonial era. It was so refreshing to be in the higher altitudes and fascinating to step back even further in Burmese time, the 1800s, when it had resembled life in most of the other countries of the region. The mode of transportation was a horse-drawn stage carriage, and a local Indian family kindly showed us all the sights: large, colorful public gardens, temples, and colonial estates. These few days were a pleasant respite from the heat and chaos of most of our time in Southeast Asia and our concerns about Julie and Ricky, but with our visas almost expired, we were compelled to head back to the craziness of Rangoon and the challenges of our new couple.

Sure enough, Julie and Ricky had married while we were separated, though the process was more complex than they had initially thought. Ricky's status remained a mystery, and there were significant hurdles to finalizing the arrangement. Rozita and I tried to share our concerns, but saw that Julie was undaunted, and we added strong-willed to her list of signature qualities. She was not going to veer from her plans with her newfound Burmese friend. Her excitement with the "temporary marriage" had only increased since we had separated.

The next challenge we all faced was having enough cash to get out of the country, as we had spent most of our money and yet needed more to pay an "exit fee" to leave legally. Ricky had the solution. Burmese citizens were not allowed to purchase certain foreign products, and there was a Diplomatic Store where only people with a Western passport could shop. Ricky negotiated with a local family friend who gave us a list of desired Western items, everything from candy to magazines to medical supplies, and the exchange would provide us with enough currency to leave the country. The shopkeeper did wonder why I was purchasing lipstick and perfume, but otherwise, buying the contraband goods for local citizens went smoothly.

We quickly completed the transactions and now, with enough Burmese currency to get to the airport, hurried off to catch a plane to Calcutta. Unfortunately, Ricky could not travel with us. The Burmese government wanted Julie and Ricky to pay $22,000 to reimburse the country for the expenses involved in educating him, since he was leaving and therefore not planning to contribute to the economy. Julie wanted to stay and help him, but overstaying her visa would only further complicate matters. What had seemed like a reasonable plan was now beyond complex.

Julie made the difficult decision to fly to India without him, promising to return when she could to find a way for Ricky to emigrate from Burma with her.

After a few days in Calcutta, we went on to Nepal, where our paths diverged. I had met some British hikers and agreed to join them on their trek in the mountains in Western Nepal, a plan of no interest to Julie and Rozita. After an amazing two weeks of trekking from Pokhara to Jomsom, I returned to Kathmandu and reconnected with my travel mates, only to find Julie in a tizzy. She could not unmarry Ricky; she felt guilty, and he was persistent about their future together. Yet the monetary and logistical hurdles to get him out of Burma continued to mount.

We shortly parted ways; I was on my way to Sri Lanka to resume my surfing journey, and I planned to keep in touch. This was a much greater challenge in the '70s without cell phones, and we never reconnected. To this day, I wonder what eventually transpired with their unique relationship. Did Ricky ever get out of Burma? Is he living in Australia with Julie? I also do not hesitate to admonish anyone who is considering marriage to help someone with their citizenship status. There are many reasons to proceed with caution!

AUTHOR'S NOTES

Burma, now known as Myanmar, is a country in Southeast Asia, located between Thailand, Bangladesh, Laos, and China. Most of these nations have different and complex border laws, which makes travel between them complicated. Burma is home to the world's longest civil war, and travel to the country in 2025 is discouraged for safety reasons.

As noted in the story, unlike its neighbors, Burma/Myanmar does not encourage tourism, and there were a number of complications to visiting, which is why, in 1977, most visitors to Asia skipped this country. However, we had heard a number of intriguing stories about life in Burma, and despite the noted challenges, our trip did not disappoint. The beauty of the country and its religious structures, coupled with its fascinating history, made it a worthwhile destination.

While we were only in Calcutta for a short time, the experience was impactful. The massive city in Eastern India was the home to Mother Teresa and, sadly, has the highest concentration of poverty in Asia. A visitor needs to prepare for the omnipresent beggars and the many other signs of people living in dire conditions. As a positive, there are many examples of organizations working to improve the quality of life, and just walking the streets of the city is an eye-opening experience.

Burmese contemporary car

Buddhist Monk at Shwedagon Pagoda

The beauty and sanctity of the pagodas

Maymyo mode of transportation

THE GOODNESS OF
PEOPLE, SRI LANKA, INDIA,
POLAND | 1977

═══════════

EVERYTHING ABOUT HIKKADUWA FELT RIGHT. A NAR-row coastal road with a number of small homes and a few commercial establishments separated a beautiful beach from the massive inland jungle. Nestled in the verdant backyard of a vibrant local character, my cottage was only a few yards from the ocean and offered easy access to delectable, cheap food, and, most importantly, a multitude of interesting travelers who provided amusement, friendship, and enlightening conversations. There were the renegade Germans from the notorious Baader-Meinhof gang with their radical stories and violent perspective on life, Palle, the softspoken, brilliant Danish philosopher who mused on Bob Dylan, D. H. Lawrence and Plato's cave, and last but not least, Pauline, who was a mother to us all, providing wisdom, life perspective and support to us in a myriad of ways. Although there were not many surfers in town, the vibe in this neighborhood suited me well.

This morning, I was feeling an uptick in positive energy from some great rides, making me believe I finally had this spot wired. The waves at the main reef were not that steep or large, but for some reason, I had been having trouble making the most of their potential. How many times had my excitement been accelerated by the hope of carving on an upcoming section, only to be disappointed by the wave's loss of energy once I was in it, making the ride a mild disappointment. Today was different, to use a surfing cliche, "I was feeling it in the surf," and for the first time in my Sri Lankan stay, I had that tremendous feeling of enjoyment in the waves.

"Harvey, are you okay?" I gazed up to see one of the other surfers looking down at me with an expression of worry and bewilderment. Why was I washing about in the shallows in such a fog, my board, still attached to my ankle, banging alternately against my torso and the omnipresent coral?

"What happened? How did I get here?" I groggily muttered.

Earlier that day, sitting in the lineup, I was feeling so good about my surfing! Astonishingly, my next awareness of myself was being washed about in the shallow white water on the shoreline. Slowly, I gained some form of consciousness. I was lying at the edge of the beach, small waves washing over me, not in pain but utterly confused, unable to get my bearings and not cognizant of how I went from the surf zone, some thirty yards offshore, to this spot on the edge of the beach.

With assistance, I staggered to my feet, gathered my board, and slowly walked the familiar path through the palm grove back to my shack, confused about what had happened but in such a weak mental and physical state that I could only focus on the task of returning home. Alone, no rinse, no taking off my suit, I flopped onto my bed. Hours later, I awoke to the familiar howl of my monkey friends. It was dark, so I knew I had been asleep for hours. I had no energy to change my clothes, eat, or do any of the usual end-of-the-day chores. I thought I should check in with someone, but the energy was not there. I drifted back into a deep slumber.

It was morning. I could feel the emerging heat of the day and heard my landlord Basil's daily, cheerful greeting, "Good morning, ocean boy; nice day." My response of a grunt caused him to poke his head through the doorway, and he sensed something was wrong.

I confirmed his concern with a weak response of "I think I need a medic." Basil showed a sense of alarm and, being such a kind soul, assured me that he would get me some help immediately.

It was a few hours before the local doctor appeared at the door. Other than Basil's word and a sketchy-looking bag, the man showed no sign of the medical profession. He performed a superficial inspection and confidently declared I had a bad case of malaria. Nervous about his diagnosis, I weakly responded that I had been taking quinine for the past year, to which he replied that there were strains that were not impacted by that treatment. Being too fatigued to argue further, I agreed to take the suggested pills, and he promised to return the next day.

The downward path of my health accelerated. Kind Basil brought me some food, but otherwise, I remained in bed, wondering how I would recover from my condition, given the circumstances. I was too weak to go out and find a friend for support or do anything to improve my condition, the feeling of helplessness adding to my health concerns and bewilderment about what had transpired in the water. The doctor returned a day later and immediately changed his diagnosis, saying now that I had typhoid fever. He gave me some antibiotics and told me not to eat for three days. My confidence in this man diminished even more, and my physical and mental reaction to my medical condition weakened me to the point that I began to lose faith in the potential for my recovery. The pain was minimal, but my drive and mental acuity seemed to be washing out to sea like the ebbing tide.

One day later, a miracle walked into my cottage. My friends, Fraser and Mary, whom I had met on the beach a few weeks prior, stopped by for a visit. They took one look at me and said, "You have hepatitis!" Not having a mirror, I was unable to see my jaundice, but Mary pulled one from her shoulder bag and held it up to me.

One look at the "yellow" whites of my eyes, coupled with my

brown urine, which I had noticed earlier, left little doubt about the diagnosis. While I did not feel better immediately, the cloud of not knowing what was wrong began to lift, and with it went some of my worry. Just as importantly, I now had trusted friends who would care for me. I was no longer alone to deal with this medical mystery.

What was hepatitis, and how was I going to recover? Months earlier in Thailand, I learned about this liver disease and a gammagoblin shot people were getting as a prophylactic. A local medical student there told me not to waste my money on the shot and just eat more carefully. I followed the first part of his advice, but my cheapness led me to be a bit careless with the second portion. Where did I pick it up? Maybe ice in a drink in India or a poorly washed piece of fruit at just about any market in my travels?

Thank goodness for my American friends, Fraser and Mary. They were seasoned Asian travelers, having lived for most of the last decade on a houseboat in Kashmir, in northern India. Most importantly, they had nursed many Western travelers back to health from a variety of diseases, and they cared!

Mary took on the maternal role, insisting on a strict diet and obvious rest. A week later, my recovery had improved, and my spirits lifted even more by a visit from Akra, a young doctor whom I had previously taught to surf. He insisted on taking me to his beautiful home in a pleasant part of the capital city of Colombo, where I enjoyed the conveniences of running water, great food, a fan, and, most importantly, a loving family who doted over me. There was a friendly competition between his mother and sisters regarding who gave me the most attention. Never had I been the recipient of such fussing!

Having a clean, pleasant environment with the attention of such loving people was boosting my recovery as well as my spirits. Unfortunately, one day, Akra informed me that there was an outbreak of malaria on the island, and if I contracted that nasty disease on top of my hepatitis, my condition would be precarious. Simultaneously, I realized my Sri Lankan visa was overextended, and I certainly could

not go to the embassy in my condition. During this period of seden-
tary recovery, I had concluded that it was time to head back to the
States. There were other places I wanted to visit and surf in Asia and
Africa, but I was mentally and physically yearning to be back home
in Philly for a variety of reasons: my health, my friends and family,
sense of life purpose, and an easier lifestyle, to name a few.

Akra concocted a plan. It was the beginning of the Muslim celebration of Ramadan, and the airport was jammed with the devoted
headed for Mecca. With all the chaos of the crowds, he thought there
was a good chance that immigration would not bother with an only
slightly overextended visa. He was right.

He helped me purchase a ticket from Sri Lanka to Bombay and
dropped me off amid the bedlam of the Colombo International Airport. The crowds, the incessant noise, and the noxious smells upset my
healing body that had grown accustomed to the serenity and support
of Akra's household. I gingerly plodded through all the chaotic exit
hoops and was eventually safely on a plane to Bombay. Akra's last bit
of important advice was not to tell anybody I had hepatitis, as I might
get impounded in the country, just one more thing to worry about.

Landing in Bombay brought on a whole new set of challenges.
The airline had lost my surfboard, and though I was willing to spend
a little money for a comfortable bed, there were no available rooms
in the city because of Ramadan. Plus, I was alone in this massive city
without any of the wonderful friends who had been caring for me
for the past month. I had been spoiled by so much attention.

Once I recovered my board, I immersed myself in the urban chaos
and eventually found an acceptable room: no bugs, relatively clean
sheets, a fan to cool me as well as drown out the omnipresent city
noise, and, most importantly, running, albeit un-drinkable, water.

First thing the next day, I began the hectic process of trying to find
an inexpensive ticket back to the US. I had experienced an amazing two
years of surfing and exploration, but my sickness was driving me to get
home asap. Talking with some other travelers about affordable tickets,

I was guided to the Aeroflot (the Soviet airline) office and purchased a ticket to New York with a short layover in Poland for only $400. However, Warsaw was behind the Iron Curtain, and as an American, I was concerned about needing papers to get through any international hurdles. The folks in Bombay said no problem. They were wrong!

I have learned there are usually catches when you get a bargain. This time, it was the fact that to get a cheap fare, I needed to spend two more days in Bombay, normally not an issue, but more of an opportunity to experience one of the more exotic, large cities of Asia. However, with my weakened health and anxiousness to get home, the prospect was not as enticing. Nonetheless, I began to explore the city, as I had so many others in the last two years. A number of fascinating conversations with locals and observations of people seeming to be happily living in appalling conditions were a distraction from my personal worries. To observe a group of naked boys cheerfully using a hole in an elevated, large, rusty container for drinking and showering gave some perspective to my own challenges. Thankfully, the days passed without any more surprises.

The trip to the airport went smoothly, and the first portion of the flight was uneventful, with no problem with customs, a relatively comfortable seat, and a fascinating layover in Dubai, but all that changed when we landed in Warsaw.

The first shock was the weather. Having spent two years in the tropics and only having clothing fit for that climate, I stepped off the plane in Poland in December, feeling a degree of cold for which I was unprepared. I quickly entered a small, drab shelter to handle immigration and customs. Within the first few minutes, the hammer fell, once again, a lost surfboard, plus being told I had to stay in this minimally heated bungalow for two days, as I had no immigration papers. This was not going to work for my hepatitis-weak body. I feebly tried to describe what a surfboard was in broken German (not initially realizing that the Polish guards were not thrilled with speaking German as a result of WWII). I filled out some papers, knowing that my cherished board, which had made it to the last leg of my round-the-world trip, would probably end up on the wall of some Polish bureaucrat's living room! It was never to be found.

Losing my beloved surfboard a second time turned out to be the least of my problems. I needed to get warm, find some food, and rest my weakened body without broadcasting my condition. The possibility of any of this happening was going nowhere when a petite, yet tough, middle-aged Polish woman came on the scene and said, "Come with me. Don't ask any questions." With no alternatives, I knew she was my best option. She escorted me through customs and immigration with only brief exchanges with the officials, all in Polish, which I obviously didn't understand, and, most importantly, into the warm portion of the terminal.

Gaining confidence and trust in this kind woman, I followed her to her car, and once inside, she explained to me in broken English that she was going to take me to a decent downtown Warsaw hotel, where I would have a free room and food.

She would pick me up in two days and return me to the airport in time for my flight. I could call a number if I wanted to tour the city, but otherwise I should keep a low profile. I was tempted to engage her with questions about how and why she managed to get me out of this mess, but sensing she was a person of few words, I simply showed her what appreciation I could and nodded to all her requests. To this day, I have no idea what her name was or for whom she worked, or why she wanted to help me. All I know is she was alerted in some way to my situation, as a foreign traveler, and stepped in and was one of the growing number of guardian angels who helped me over the past month.

My journey was now on a more positive path. The hotel was warm, comfortable, and clean. The first bit of luxury was running a hot bath, my first in two years. I turned on a radio in the room and found a station that was playing unrecognizable music, but I left it on, listening out of curiosity. Then, as I settled into the hot, soapy water, the song "Speedy Gonzalez" began to play. I had to smile.

After all I had been through in the past few weeks, here I was, comfortably relaxing in a lovely hotel bath in Warsaw, Poland, listening to Pat Boone's humorous song of my youth with words that seemed fitting for my predicament: "Come on home to your adobe / And slap some mud on the wall / The roof is leakin' like a strainer / There's loads of roaches in the hall…"

Life only got better. The meals in the hotel were robust, safe to eat, and my first "western cuisine" since Australia. Feeling a bit stronger, I took advantage of the tours and walked a bit in the local neighborhood, getting a sense of the tumultuous history of this region. As I enjoyed these peaceful few days, I did keep wondering about my savior: for whom did she work, how did she have that authority, how did she know about me? None of these questions were ever answered.

Sure enough, two days later, she returned, picked me up outside the hotel at the agreed-upon time, and escorted me through the various departure hurdles, all with virtually no superfluous conversation, just the minimum which had to be shared to get me through my exit from Poland. We parted ways with me showering her with words of appreciation, but with no more answers to my questions about her story. I hopefully showed sufficient gratitude for her efforts.

I felt a euphoric relief as the plane rose above the city, and the pilot explained in English our flight plans to New York, where my girlfriend Sherry and my parents awaited my return. All I had to do was sit on this plane, eat some familiar food, and relax; no squabbling in foreign languages, no worries about where I would sleep or eat, and, most importantly, no stress about my prospects of being medically evaluated by a competent American doctor.

As is typical in life, just when you let your guard down, adversity shows up on your doorstep. About an hour into the flight, a middle-aged Polish woman sitting next to me, who had previously shared in broken English that this was her first plane trip, began to violently throw up. She filled up her bag and asked me for mine. I felt bad for her and offered her support, just when I thought I was finished with the exotic smells of Asia! The lingering impact of my hepatitis, combined with the odor from my seatmate's retching, did not sit well with me. Fortunately, there were enough vacant spots on the flight that the attendants were able to move her to a distant row.

I reentered my state of calm for about an hour when suddenly the plane began to shudder with constant upward and downward movements, something my stomach did not appreciate. After a tumultuous few minutes, the captain announced that all would be fine, but we were making an emergency landing. What other calamity could possibly come my way?

Our destination was a small, remote airport in northern Canada. As we bounced along the thin, icy runway, all I could see was snow and a small terminal. The captain informed us that since we would be here for a while, we had the option of going to the building or staying seated. The plane was warm. There was food. I was going nowhere.

After a few hours filled with questions and worry, we departed the frigid airport, headed for New York. Before long, I joined the many passengers who felt a sense of relief at the sight of the Statue of Liberty, and as we began our descent to JFK, the sense of familiarity infused me with energy.

Spotting Sherry and my parents once we were in the terminal, I felt a final release from this perilous end of my journey. They were excited to see me, but I sensed their visible concern at my haggard, sickly countenance. Little did they know what hurdles I had just encountered just to get home and how many guardian angels I had been blessed with in the last month.

Upon arriving in Philadelphia, one of the first things I did was weigh myself. I had dropped from 170 to 130 pounds, almost my high school wrestling weight class. As in Sri Lanka, I was underwhelmed with the American medical care, but I should have known that a suburban Philadelphia doctor would not be an expert on tropical diseases, though he was a few steps ahead of my friendly physician in Hikkaduwa.

After the Christmas holidays, which had afforded me an opportunity to reconnect with family and friends, the transition from almost two years in third-world countries to my former life was a bit overwhelming. I could tell that folks were alarmed by both my sickly, slowly recovering countenance and my social awkwardness that developed once I returned to the United States. I was relieved to be home, but my travels had left me unsettled with the more elaborate elements of first-world living. Some aspects of American life now seemed foreign to me, and this manifested itself primarily in social situations. Attempting to summarize such an amazing experience in a few words, recognizing the challenges of returning to such a rich country after living primarily in the third world for so long, was difficult, even with friends who knew me well. Many questions were running through my head, and I yearned for some peace of mind.

In January, I made the mistake of going back to work at my old school, too soon. Reconnecting as the wrestling coach felt awkward. I knew and loved the sport and had worked with many of the athletes before my trip, but while there were familiar coaching moments of excitement, joy, and frustration, I knew something was not right.

After the season ended in March, I took a job with a landscaping company, and the outdoor work provided an environment more conducive to my state of mind. Planting trees and cutting grass offered a respite from dealing with the culture shock of returning home. By summer, things began to feel normal once more, but the Sri Lanka-India-Poland ordeal had left a lasting stamp on my persona. I recognized how dependent and connected we are with our family and friends, and that I needed to do more to help others now that I had been the recipient of such generosity. Perhaps part of my challenge to adjust to American life was not just my sickness but the timing of my return at Christmas, where the lavish decorations and attention on material goods collided with what I had grown accustomed to during my journey through third-world countries.

While my international experience had allowed me to grow in

innumerable ways, returning home was not easy, and as many long-term travelers find, my perspective had changed. Fortunately, time is a great healer, and the unsettled feeling was a small price to pay for my incredible "gift of experience."

AUTHOR'S NOTES

Hikkaduwa is a small fishing village about fifty miles south of Colombo, the capital of the island nation of Sri Lanka. The former British colony is just below India and is influenced significantly by the monsoon seasons, with each side of the island having a rainy season for half the year and a dry period for the remainder. The surf is impacted by the monsoon, with each side having a season of large swells and one when the ocean is relatively flat. I obviously went to the side with the larger waves, and Hikkaduwa was the one town with a few open-air restaurants and guesthouses that catered to Western travelers.

The political climate was also an influential variable in my time there. During the 1970s, there was some instability in the country due to the clash between the Hindu Tamils and the Buddhist Sinhalese. Most of the fighting was in the north of the country, but there was some tension between the two ethnic groups everywhere, which was a source of concern, even for foreigners.

I had come overland from India and arrived in the country following extensive travel through eastern Asia, with my first challenge being retrieving my surfboard that I had shipped from Singapore months earlier. Traveling through Asia is difficult enough, so I was advised to not have the burden of a surfboard unless I planned to use it a lot. I was pleasantly surprised when I found the appropriate warehouse amid the chaos of Colombo, and a worker emerged with my cherished board. Up until my major health issue, I found life there enlightening as well as relatively easy.

Bombay, now called Mumbai, is one of the largest cities in India with a population exceeding twelve million. It is compared to New York, as it has a major entertainment and financial industry. Like most large Asian cities, there is a first-world or third-world feel depending on the section of the city. Mumbai faces a major challenge of income inequality, as it is home to the largest number of billionaires in Asia, yet also to some of the poorest communities in India. My time there was brief, but I quickly observed the reality of income inequality.

Swimming pool, bath, and water fountain in Bombay

The cheering section from the beach in Hikkaduwa

ENCOUNTERING APARTHEID,
SOUTH AFRICA | 1983

═══════════

I HAD JUST TAKEN A LEAK, AND AS I RETURNED TO THE
benches in the middle of the expansive, yet empty, waiting room
where Louisa was sleeping, I was shocked to see four soldiers, dressed
in full-length army green coats with guns slung over their shoulders.
Louisa poked her head up, half-asleep but obviously nervous about
the soldiers' intent. My mind exploded from drowsiness to panic, as
Louisa and I stared at each other, not knowing how to react to this
alarming intrusion into our "newlywed suite."

It was 1983, and we were spending the first night of our honeymoon travels in the Johannesburg railway station. Having landed
earlier that evening, missing the last train to the coast, and wanting
to catch an early one the next day, we decided it was silly to pay for
a hotel room for just a few hours' rest. I had spent many a night in
similar venues around the world, and this station had seemed relatively safe with a fair bit of activity at this late hour.

Louisa and I had chosen South Africa for our honeymoon for
a variety of reasons. Selfishly, since my round-the-world surf trip
was cut short by my bout with hepatitis, I was eager to get back on
route and surf the great waves along its Indian Ocean coastline. At
the same time, the World Surfing Tour was making its first-ever stop
in South Africa, and I was hoping to surf with some of the world's

best in these great waves. In addition, a South African teaching colleague in Philadelphia raved about the many other attractions in her country, such as the game reserves and the beauty of the diverse landscapes. Louisa, at twenty-three, had a growing passion for travel after her previous summer solo backpack trip through Europe, and while cautious, was excited to learn from the ten-year advantage I had on her with my previous world travels.

The flip side of our decision was the controversy due to the country's policy of apartheid, resulting in our country's sanctions and divestment. We experienced this conflict at home before we had even set foot in South Africa. Some of our friends questioned our plan because they felt that by traveling there, we were showing tacit support for apartheid.

When we landed in Johannesburg airport, one of the professional surfers on the flight, someone I admired a great deal, turned to me, as we exited the cabin, and said, "Harvey, you are entering my country of South Africa. It is a wonderful place, but remember: you can take the baboon out of the bush, but you can't take the bush out of the baboon. Be careful." Subsequently, during our customs inspection, we learned that we could not enter Kenya the last week of our trip as planned, for once we had a South African stamp on our passport, we were not welcome there. This nation was considered a continental pariah. Unsettled by both these exchanges, Louisa and I quickly had the realization that we would constantly be assessing our connection with apartheid and the resulting consequences of such a policy in the upcoming months. There would be some sensitive moments ahead related to this complex issue and our relationship with the people we would meet.

From the airport, we explored Johannesburg for a late-night dinner. While there was a range of restaurant options, the "Whites Only" signs at the entrances subdued our hunger and enhanced our misgivings. We finally chose a simple eatery that offered a variety of local foods. While the cuisine itself was fine, the company was more problematic. We could not help but overhear the conversations around us. It was clear that the people in this eatery were not only comfortable with the apartheid policies but happy with them. Hearing this seemingly genteel clientele make jokes about blacks showed us even more clearly the moral and emotional complexities that we would witness in South Africa in the next few months.

At that nerve-wracking moment in the waiting room, wishing I had gotten a hotel room rather than sleeping in the train station, I rushed to engage with the soldiers at Louisa's side. But they were Afrikaner and did not speak much English. At first, I hesitated, having never faced armed soldiers who were obviously not pleased with our sleeping choice for the evening. Then, working to diffuse the situation as clearly as I could in simple English, I explained we were American teachers and were excited to spend our honeymoon and summer vacation traveling in their country.

Their response was simply, "Come with us." We had no alternative but to follow the command. My loss of control of the situation was deeply concerning to me, as I was the greatest advocate for this trip, and I was the more experienced traveler. We gathered up our gear and followed behind our new acquaintances, not saying a word of opposition to their bidding.

We finally halted at the railway police office and subsequently witnessed a group of visibly terrified, bloodied, and dirty black prisoners being roughly pushed into a cell. Their treatment unnerved us even more. It reminded me of the images I had seen of the Red Summer of 1919, where the white-on-black violence in the United States was at its peak.

Once the prisoners were taken care of, the soldiers were now having a serious, lengthy conversation in Afrikaans, which we assumed was focused on what to do with us American newlyweds. The one who seemed to be in charge finally turned to us and said, "You will come with me." Louisa and I followed him out of the building and into his car, not daring to question his request but continuing to be nervous about our next destination. Our backpacks and my surf-board were left behind. As unsettled as this progression of the evening had been, we felt there was no option to resist their plan for us.

As we drove out of the lot, our new "friend," Jenny, seemed to lighten up a bit and spoke in choppy English. He explained that it was not safe to spend the night in the train station. As evidence, he shared that recently there had been several murders in the waiting room where we had been sleeping, so he was taking us to his apartment. Jenny went on to explain that he had to go back to work, but he wanted to share breakfast with us when he finished his shift. He deposited us in his living room on a sofa bed and headed back to the station.

After Jenny left, we caught our breath and looked wide-eyed at each other, unable to fully communicate what we were thinking. His wife was present in the nearby bedroom, and the space was quite small with only a kitchen, bedroom, living room, and bathroom. Talking was completely out of the question, as we feared she might hear us, and sleep was a priority as a result of the fatigue from the long flight, jet lag, and the unsettling events in the train station. Although Jenny had warmed up to us, we both felt a nervous uncertainty regarding what lay ahead in the morning.

We slept restlessly until hearing his wife depart at sunrise, as Jenny mentioned she would, and sure enough, a few hours later, he returned with a bag of groceries. He firmly handed it to Louisa with the directive to cook breakfast, while he and I moved to the balcony of his apartment. I could only imagine my new wife's frame of mind, given his commanding words and body language, and her having to work with unfamiliar food in a foreign kitchen after the bizarre night we had just experienced. What had I gotten my bride into?

Once we were outside, he pulled out a scrapbook to show me, in his words, pictures of "hunting gorillas." The images were not of animals in trees of the jungle, but rather Angolan rebels. As generous and pleasant as Jenny seemed, it was obvious that he felt apartheid was necessary for his survival in the world as he knew it, a world where he had the power to do what he thought was "right."

It was my first experience of being careful with my words regarding apartheid. I felt torn between my feelings of gratitude for how Jenny was helping us and unease regarding his racist perspective. I was appalled by his pictures and description of "hunting gorillas," wondering his purpose in showing me the album. At the same time, I could see his determination to protect life as he knew it. He had never known anything but apartheid, and because South Africa was surrounded by black ruled countries that challenged the rule of the white government, he felt threatened. In his mind, he was protecting his nation.

After our breakfast of various meats and eggs, Jenny returned us to the railway station. When we entered the departure area, an attendant approached us and said, "You must be the Zendts." From there, we were quickly escorted to our coach.

Jenny had arranged for first-class tickets to Port Elizabeth with our stored backpacks and surfboard already on board. While pleasantly surprised, we remained confused by this special treatment and our lack of payment. We were rushed to jump on board, as the train was departing shortly, and despite our offering, they would not take any money from us to pay our fare. This was just the first instance of the incredible South African hospitality, seemingly wanting us to have a good impression of their country, possibly from knowing of their poor international reputation.

We were now eager to see beyond what we had experienced in our first twenty-four hours in this country. We had witnessed a bit of the underbelly, the part of South Africa that we knew existed but had never experienced firsthand, the part whites might want to keep hidden from foreigners who oppose their laws that enforced racial discrimination. I kept wondering if we were treated this way because we were white and American. This was just the beginning of many fascinating insights into this complex issue during our two-month stay in the country.

The scenic ride to the coast was disrupted by intermittent evidence of apartheid: the racially segregated train stations and neighborhoods as well as the omnipresent signage: "Bus stop for nonwhites," "Europeans Only," "Native Bus Stop," "Beware of Natives," and for public telephones "Public Telephone" and "African Telephone" to name a few. As a history teacher, I knew the fundamental principles of apartheid and its stringent laws. For example, the Bantu Labor Act denied black workers the right to live with their families in white areas, and the Immorality Act prohibited sexual relations between whites and other races. However, it was one thing to read about these practices in a book. It was another to witness how apartheid impacted the daily lives of these people. We continued to be unsettled by the injustice of this system; yet at the same time, we were awestruck by the natural beauty of the country and the friendliness of the people, both black and white.

Arriving in the coastal city of Port Elizabeth that afternoon, we were ready to test the roads for hitchhiking. I had plenty of experiences by the side of the road in many different countries and venues, but I was a bit apprehensive about hitchhiking in this complicated country with rules that I had already violated, namely sleeping in the train station. This uneasiness was enhanced by the fact that we did not see anyone else engaged in this activity.

Although Louisa was new to hitchhiking, she trusted my judgement. It was still early in our marriage! We found it easy to get a ride to Jeffrey's Bay, a coastal town with arguably the best right point break in the world. Setting up our tent, overlooking the Indian Ocean, we absorbed ourselves in the natural beauty of this coastal area, free from the confusing, manmade laws that made no sense to us. I spent the afternoon in the ocean, and Louisa took long walks, and with the watercolors she brought from home, immersed herself in capturing the beauty of the coast in her sketchbook.

As surfers know, riding waves forces you to direct your attention completely to the present surroundings. In fact, it is dangerous not to put yourself in that mind-clearing, meditative, dissociative state, especially with waves as powerful as the ones at Jeffrey's Bay. Out in the ocean, away from the signage and constant reminders of apartheid, I was able to lose myself in this outstanding surf. I was amazed to discover that the amount of time it took to ride a single wave at Jeffrey's Bay was longer than the cumulative time surfing an entire afternoon in New Jersey! This experience was the main reason I had wanted to come to this country initially, and I was already feeling rewarded in my first session in the water.

Yet, once back on land, the intermittent evidence of apartheid kept the unsettling feeling regarding this issue continuously on my mental "back burner." While hesitant to share my political perspective with just anyone, I made a point of striking up conversations with both blacks and whites when it seemed appropriate, trying always to be careful not to cross any lines that might be deemed offensive or judgmental.

Our primary mode of transportation was hitchhiking, and as the weeks went by, Louisa and I became more experienced in navigating the tricky topic of racial discrimination with total strangers. Invariably, when drivers picked us up, they would ask our impressions of their beloved country. Since we were in their car and did not want to offend them, we would begin our response with all the positives, while attempting to size up where they stood on this controversial issue, and tempering our responses accordingly. While apartheid was rarely mentioned initially, the conversation often ended up on the topic. Most South Africans would be very candid with their perspective. Ironically, some of the nicest people we met felt that apartheid was necessary for the survival of their country.

We discovered quickly that contrasting views on apartheid were not delineated solely by race. As an example, Flicky and Bruce, cousins of our British South African friend in Philadelphia, invited us and another white couple to stay with them at their beach cottage on the Wild Coast. Flicky and Bruce were from Cape Town but chose to live in the Transkei, one of the black homelands, partially because of their opposition to apartheid. They taught at the University of Umtata, now called Walter Sisulu University, named after the anti-apartheid activist. They wanted to raise their children in a community where there was little segregation. Here, one did not see the "whites only" signs and other visible reminders of apartheid.

In contrast, the other couple had emigrated from Zimbabwe because of the changes to their country when it ended its racist policies. They had feared for their safety as well as for their comfortable standard of living in their former homeland. This couple referred to themselves as "When wes" because they were expatriates who talked nostalgically about their former homes and lifestyle in colonial Africa. The "When wes" felt their life had been ruined by the end of Zimbabwe's brand of apartheid, and they were worried that South Africa would have the same results if it ended its policy. In contrast, Flicky and Bruce felt that apartheid was immoral and needed to be ended, no matter what the economic and social consequences. While these two couples were friends, their contrasting views clearly captured the complexity of the issue.

Though Louisa and I certainly aligned with Flicky and Bruce, most of our contributions to the conversations were questions rather than opinions. We felt a multitude of reactions, both positive and negative, to the difficult decisions the "When wes" faced when they decided to leave Zimbabwe. On one hand, we felt some empathy that the "When wes" were forced to abandon their way of life and had trouble figuring out how to take their savings with them because the government allowed emigrating citizens to take only $1000 at a time. This limit was to prevent Zimbabwe's economy from tanking. On the other hand, we felt some disgust with the methods the "When wes" used for getting around the "unfair" laws. The irony of their outrage over the questionable regulations did not escape us.

One example of the lengths the "When wes" went to keep their wealth is as ingenious as it is repugnant, and it involved making money from the oil embargo. They were part of a group that leased large container cars for trains, filled them with oil in the neighboring country of Mozambique, but plugged the section that was to be checked at the border with molasses. The border inspectors would not know about the oil because all they found was molasses in that section, letting them through, whereby they could sell the oil at a huge profit. They took their oil proceeds and purchased Land Rovers in Zimbabwe, which they subsequently would drive into South Africa and sell, gaining the earnings. We marveled at their ingenuity and drive, even if we questioned facets of their rationale for the creative, complex plan.

While the weekend dialogue didn't change our opinion regarding apartheid, it certainly enhanced our understanding of the various factors regarding the policy. We admired Flicky and Bruce for the sacrifices they were making to live with their convictions and the "When wes" for their drive to adjust to the complexities of their homeland.

There are a number of somewhat warranted stereotypes regarding the two main white ethnic groups of the country, the British and the Afrikaners. Visiting our South African colleague's family in Cape Town, we experienced the point of view of the privileged and reasoned perspective of an elderly lawyer and his lovely, engaged wife. These South African Brits were mostly antiapartheid, but we learned over dinner with their friends to be wary of stereotyping South African Brits and Dutch Afrikaners, who were viewed as mostly in favor of the policy. We found it easy to share our feelings honestly with this interesting couple and recognized the danger of making generalizations in this deeply diverse country.

Back on the road, leaving Cape Town, we were picked up by an affluent Afrikaner farmer, who persuaded us to stay the night on his plantation north of the city. Little English was spoken, but his unanticipated hospitality was most generous, treating us with fresh grapes, amazing wine, and a spectacular South African "braai," a tradition of grilling meat over an open fire outside, in a handsome stone fireplace. We left with bags of plump raisins and muffins stuffed in our backpacks and many unanswered questions. The family was eager to show us their farm and treated us so warmly. Their hospitality, coupled with the language barrier, led us to the decision to stay away from political discussion during our stay, and we left without knowing their take on apartheid. Why were these people so generous? They seemed anxious or determined to share their humanity with us. Once again, we wondered if it was because we were white Americans, or were they just simply generous, good people?

Our last weeks in South Africa were spent in a rental car, driving north to Durban, a large metropolitan area and port on the Indian Ocean coast settled by British Indian laborers, and then further north to Kruger National Park to experience the amazing wildlife of the country. En route, we were invited to visit a friend of Flicki's, Philip, a black preacher. He lived with his family outside Pietermaritzburg in a small, unique area where blacks could own property and had some freedoms not found elsewhere in the country. Here, they could travel without constant fear of the police, engage freely with people of all races, and live without the constant reminders of the country's controversial policies. In the early 1900s, a missionary sold land to some black farmers and created this small township. Since this was instituted before apartheid, the residents were allowed to keep this arrangement and maintain these unique freedoms.

Phillip was a gracious host, but when he introduced us to anyone in his congregation, he made clear that we were Americans, assuring that nobody would think that he was getting too close to white South Africans. There was a raw honesty and awkwardness to the experience. Philip asked us, "Why are you visiting me?" We were truthful in our response; friends had said it was one of the few ways to understand how blacks live in the country. Despite the relative peacefulness of his local community, Philip shared that he saw a racial revolution on the horizon and was very worried about their future. Ironically, he was under the impression that blacks had it great in America, and we enlightened him a bit on the racial realities in our country.

There were other memorable moments that enhanced our understanding of apartheid. In a restaurant that served all races, near one of the homeland borders, we observed that blacks had to bring their own cutlery while whites were given all the silverware they needed. When asking a fellow customer about the practice, he explained that the owners feared theft from the nonwhite customers but trusted the whites.

One of our longest rides hitchhiking was in the back of a bottle truck with a number of black workers. Since there was constant noise, we could not engage in any meaningful conversation with our "truck mates." However, we were subtly entertained by watching the surprised expressions on the faces of the white drivers passing us on the highway, observing this rare interracial connection.

Safety was an issue. It was obvious when watching the news and talking to people that concern about crime was a major worry for all South Africans. There had recently been some major riots protesting apartheid, and while the majority of incidents occurred in the black townships, there was frequent evidence of security precautions by many whites, locked gates, guards, etc., everywhere.

In one campground on the beach in East London, which was near one of the black townships, the owner said it was safe for us to camp one night because of other visitors being there. However, the following evening, he would not let us remain in a tent once the other campers left, insisting that we move into one of the guest-houses, which could be locked. He simply said it was not safe to be in the open alone. We appreciated this gesture but were surprised by his intense concern for our safety.

With the exception of the first night in the train station, we felt safe in the myriad of diverse situations on our trip.

Louisa and I had a wonderful time in this country, meeting amazing people, visiting some beautiful areas, seeing unique wildlife, and, for me, surfing some great waves, but the shadow of apartheid always loomed over us in some manner. We left South Africa with an enhanced understanding of the complexity and realities of apartheid, and we concluded that the country would not survive this policy without significant bloodshed. We were surprised and relieved when, out of the blue, or so it seemed, Nelson Mandela was released from prison and white rule ended in the 1990s.

AUTHOR'S NOTES

South Africa, for centuries, was home to a number of strong tribal kingdoms, but in the late 1600s, British, Dutch, and German settlers arrived, and over the next two centuries, they fought for control of this valuable land. The British settled in the coastal regions while the Dutch, called Boers, moved inland. During the beginning of the 1900s, restrictive laws were imposed on the black population, leading to the institution of apartheid in the late 1940s. People were designated as either white, black, or colored (mostly Indians) with specific laws and freedoms for each group. One of its most noticeable facets was the establishment of homelands, the only areas where blacks could own land and travel freely.

Local and international backlash to this policy eventually led to its downfall in the early 1990s, and the country has a multiracial government today, though many consequential issues remain.

Situated on the southern tip of the continent, it is one of the most beautiful countries in the world. Famous for its wildlife reserves and natural beauty, it draws many international visitors. The surfers in the movie, *The Endless Summer*, went to all the great breaks around the world and found the best waves near Jeffrey's Bay in South Africa. Both the Atlantic and Indian Ocean coastlines are filled with ideal, spectacular beaches, and today surfers come from all over the world to enjoy the waves. The one negative reality is the abundance of deadly sharks, particularly on The Wild Coast, where attacks are frequent. While I loved the waves there, I constantly kept my eyes open for any nearby fins.

The wildlife reserves are the most popular attraction for visitors. Although one cannot get out of a vehicle for obvious safety reasons, you can drive through the parks and observe most of the famous animals of the African savannah. There is an unbelievable thrill to coming around a corner and observing a herd of giraffes or a pride of lions by the side of the road. At sunset, all visitors need to be inside a fenced compound or out of the park. We witnessed the rationale for this regulation when a couple was late to the compound and had to leave their unattended car outside the fence for the night. When they returned to their auto in the morning, all four tires were flat as the hyenas had chewed up the rubber!

Jenny, our host the first night
in South Africa

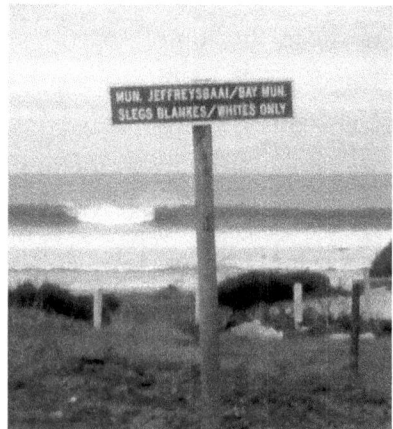

"Whites Only"
A common reminder of apartheid

The beautiful waves of Jeffreys Bay. Note there are no race signs here. The fellow with the white hat was the only Black person I ever saw on a beach, but he was careful not to draw attention to himself.

The back of the bottle truck

Philip and his wife in front of his church

Saying goodbye in Capetown, on the road again

MY FATHER'S STORY, ASIA AND THE SOUTH PACIFIC | 1935

THE INSPIRATION FOR MY TRAVELS CAME FROM MY father, who traveled extensively around the South Pacific and Asia in 1935. In honor of his adventurous spirit, I share the following two summaries of his travels; the first one he wrote for his college magazine, and the second is a vivid diary entry sharing more details about his mishap in Rarotonga, Cook Islands.

"The mysterious east! At my desk in a Philadelphia bank, I dreamed of it. Brother Lowell Thomas's book, "The Land of the Black Pagoda," fanned my curiosity to the breaking point. Converting every nickel I had into traveller's cheques, it was on to the Orient for me."

In October 1935, I sailed for Japan and spent several nights at The Florida, a ten-cent-a-dance place, where we romped to the familiar tunes of *Diana* in the *St. Louis Blues* played by an American colored Orchestra. One afternoon, I played football with Joe's European friends in the Yokohama Athletic Club against a club of fleet-footed Nipponese. It was bitterly played, and only our edge in weight saved us from an embarrassing defeat.

But winter was creeping on, and I had visions of the tropics, so I traveled down through China to French Indochina. It was in Saigon that I learned of the wily beast called the Gaur, a top prize of all big game hunters and one of the most difficult to shoot.

While on the boat to Saigon, I met a New Yorker who invited me to join him on a shooting expedition into the interior of Annam, in search of this beast. It was a great experience in the jungle, where tigers, wild boars, water buffaloes, and deer flourished, although it was in a country that probably has the meanest climate in the world. We met a French Planter who provided us with thirteen native trackers, and we trudged for a month through the sun-baked, fever-ridden, leech-laden, tiger-infested jungle. Usually, the gaur's haunts were in the most inaccessible parts where no white man had ever been. At night, the air cooled off, and we huddled near roaring log fires, which kept us from becoming dinner for the local tigers.

At times, it was a hard life in a hot, treacherous country; yet it resulted in such a huge, successful romantic adventure with shootings of banting, boar, deer, peacocks, and the treasured gaur that offset any of the discomforts.

After seeing the ghostly ruins of the Khmers at Angkor and the hundreds of Gilded temples of Bangkok in Siam, I went down the Malay Peninsula and sailed from Penang for India, on the voyage to Calcutta. I met three men who, like myself, wanted to see as much of the country as possible within a limited time. Though we merely skimmed over it, we covered some 6000 miles. The high spots were Darjeeling for Mount Everest, Allahabad for a religious melay of three million Hindus, Agra for the Taj, Delhi for its modern government buildings, Peshawar for its bazaars and the Khyber Pass, Bombay for the Parsee and their towers of silence, Hyderabad for its caves, then south to Medora and Monopoly for their temples, then to restful Ceylon.

From Colombo, I sailed east, touched Singapore, lived a month in Java and Bali, then south to Australia. Sydney was celebrating its annual fair, and to get away from the crowds, two Englishmen and I went north to the Blue Mountains for golf and hiking. Later, I left with the intention of spending some time on that most famous of South Sea Islands, Tahiti.

But the best laid plans of mice and men go awry. While ashore on the astonishingly beautiful island of Rarotonga, I was left stranded when the monthly mail boat cut short its freight discharge and was underway (with all my belongings) before I knew it. With neither money nor luggage, I lived contentedly in a picturesque palm-fronded hut among the amiable Maori natives—two months of feasting, fishing, singing, tennis, or simply bumming. It was like an extra dividend on a glorious holiday, but two months later, my luggage and money arrived on a returning mail boat, and I reluctantly sailed on to Tahiti.

For want of adventure, a Canadian chap and I sailed on a small trading schooner to a tiny uninhabited isle called Mojito, where we lived among dreamy palms, wild goats, and pineapples "a la Robinson Crusoe." Our purpose in going was to wrap tin plates around the palm trees to keep the rats from climbing up and chewing off all the coconuts. Actually, we spent more time fishing off the colorful rocky shore, but this ended too suddenly, almost tragically, when my friend was swept from a rock by a powerful wave, sucked under, and bashed on the mounds of razor-edged poisonous coral. Only his unusual strength enabled him to struggle to a nearby rock where I dragged him, limp and blood smeared from the angry waves. Fortunately, two days later, the regular trading schooner sailed close to the island; we hailed it and were taken back to Tahiti, where his wounds were properly dressed by a doctor.

But pressure from home and shrinking working capital compelled me to carry on. Reaching San Francisco. I transshipped to see the Panama Canal, Colombia, and Cuba.

For the years' time. The score is roughly this: fourteen ships, seventeen countries, 40,000 miles. My personal opinions are that Japan is the most industrious, India the most fascinating, Java the cleanest, Bali the most charming, and the South Seas the "tops."

Rarotonga (from my father's diary, unedited)

Arriving there on Sunday morning, we saw a small green island with a center ridge of jagged peaks clothed to the top with dense green foliage. But the sea was still rough, and there were no moorings; it was impossible to hold anchorage on the hard coral reefs below. For three days, we sailed back and forth like a hungry fish with that charming island less than a mile away but inaccessible to us. The monotony was exasperating.

Finally, on Wednesday morning, word was passed that we could go ashore, that they would be unloading cargo all day. While the island had no particular attraction other than its obvious beauty, I leaped at the opportunity of getting ashore and made ready. A middle-aged lady acquaintance asked that I trade some unnecessary personals for native curios, while another asked me to call for her mail.

Though the first officer told us that we could go ashore at our own risk, I concluded he meant the risk of the rough seas. So, asking one of the native foremen how long they would be unloading, he replied until 8 p.m., maybe midnight. Satisfied that everything was okay, another gentleman and I climbed down the ship's ladder into a cargo tender below. We were soon pulled ashore, and I was off to attend my errands.

Once completed, I asked a native to row me out to a beautiful schooner and was entertained by its Danish skipper for the remainder of the afternoon. Reaching the cabin, we sat down for a chat, and soon I was admiring a rather unique mirror which had at its base the rim of a ship's porthole. "That was taken from Van Luckner's ship," he said," though he did a lot of damage around these parts during the war, he was a game fellow. Sometimes we can't help admiring such people even though they are the enemy."

About that same time, a sailor entered the cabin, stating Manganui had gone. Thinking she was taking another one of her turns, I took a look out the porthole and noticed she was a bit far out to sea. Getting a bit disturbed, I headed back to shore and asked a native merchant peering through a telescope about the ship's path. He confirmed it was gone.

There I was, stranded with all my money and provisions locked in a trunk on the ship, wearing shorts and an old coat, and with about three dollars' worth of Tahitian Francs in my pocket.

Traveler Speaks To Exchangeites

George B. Zendt Tells of Life and Customs in Lands of Orient

George B. Zendt, world traveler and a brother of the local Civic Little theatre's Harvey Zendt, last night delivered an illustrated lecture of a recent tour he made of Asia and the islands of the Pacific at a meeting of the Exchange club at the Hotel Allen.

Mr. Zendt journeyed on 14 different ships on this tour. Last night he told of Japan and China and of the religions of the Orient. He said that even small children wear military garb in these countries. He elaborated in his description of the international settlement in Shanghai.

He told of the homes of French-Indo China, which are built on stilts as a protection to inhabitants from wild animals. He discussed Burma, saying that Buddha statues can be found in a thousand postures there.

India and the Ganges river were spoken of and Mr. Zendt compared the religions of the Buddhists and Hindus with those of other Orientals. He told of the wonders of Mt. Everest, which is 29,000 feet high.

GEO. ZENDT TOLD ABOUT TRAVELS AROUND WORLD

North Penn Man Marooned On Island in South Sea

PICTURES WERE SHOWN

Sellersville, Sept. 4—First hand information describing how he was marooned on a South Sea island three months with only a suit of clothes and how he traveled 40,000 miles through 17 countries featured an address delivered Thursday night by George Zendt, Jr., Souderton bond broker, before the Sellersville Kiwanis Club.

Mr. Zendt thrilled local Kiwanians as he gave this description of his vacation trip. He left Souderton recently on an aimless jaunt around the world, having no particular destination, but intending to go most everywhere. He visited all the important nations on the globe, and experienced the thrill of a lifetime on a tiny spot in the South Seas. On an island

The building of our hunting shelter

The hunt for Gaur in IndoChina

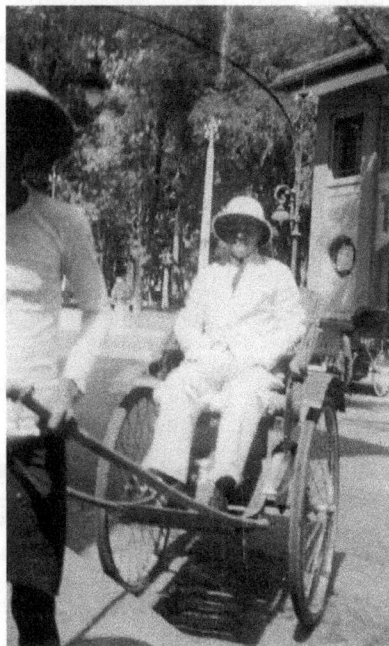

Saigon street travel

RECOGNITION AND
APPRECIATION

———

A FEW FRIENDS ALONG THE WAY WHO IMMEASURABLY enhanced my experiences.

Ben and Surrander, my hosts in Penang, Malaysia, who went out of their way to provide a memorable experience, Fall 1977.

Cedric, a South African traveling salesman who escorted us through the Garden Route along the Indian Ocean coast, Summer 1983.

Doug M, a great surfer from Florida who, along with his wife Eileen, traveled with me for five months through Central America and Hawaii. We first met in Mexico in 1974, and I visited him at his home in Costa Rica a number of times.

Doug T, my trekking partner from England, who hiked through the Himalayas with me, October 1977.

Frasier and Mary, an adventurous couple from Idaho who were my friends and saviors in Sri Lanka, Fall 1977.

Hilder, our hostess in Western Samoa, Spring 1977.

Howard, a surfer from Texas who went through the South Pacific, New Zealand, and Australia with me, Spring 1977.

Rodney, Jim, Chip, and Heps, childhood and college friends who were part of the beach crew in Puerto Rico, and on numerous trips to Mexico and Central America, 1969-1973.

Rozita, an Australian who was a seasoned traveler and was with me throughout most of the Asian portion of the trip, Fall 1977.

Sachigra and Mick, good friends from the crew at the Krishna Restaurant, where I lived and worked in Australia, Spring 1977.

Sherry, my girlfriend at the time, who was with us in Central America, Hawaii, and then visited me in Australia and Bali, 1976-1977.

Tom, a close friend from college who was with me on the trip across the country in the summer of 1970. He grew up in Hawaii and was my partner during our stay there throughout the winter of 1977.

Unknown, a mysterious and generous Polish woman, to whom I am forever grateful, who rescued me in the Warsaw airport, as I traveled home without documents, hiding my condition of hepatitis, December 1977.

Vicki, Colleen, Zoria, Barb, Lindsay, and Bob, adventurous Canadians who were with me throughout my South Pacific travels, Spring 1977.

My Jersey surfing mates over the years: the original crew, **Pete, Harry and Cutty; Jay, Wiggy and Bob** who were close in the early years and on many Hatteras trips; the 8th Street Jetty gang and generations of **Pellinis, Richmonds, Sennhenns, Kaiers, Peaces** and **Ternnoskys;** foul weather friend **Jim; Kutsy; Dave, Bob, Charlie and the rest of the Oregon crew;** Longport, NJ family friend and pro surfer **Steve Dwyer;** and my children **Peter, Becca** and **Christy.**

And, of course, **Louisa**, my loving wife, who traveled with me in South Africa on our honeymoon in the summer of 1983.

There were many others who impacted me in countless ways throughout my travels. They hosted me in their homes, showed me great surf breaks, gave me rides, shared insights and reflections, gave me direction when I needed it, and provided so many laughs and profound memories.

Finally, I must thank my friend **Darcy**, who read and edited many of my stories. She cheered me on and encouraged me to complete this project.

Harvey Zendt has always loved the ocean. Growing up in Philadelphia and spending as much time as he could on the Jersey coast, he developed a love for surfing at an early age. In the early '60s, he was part of the first surf crew at a small beach town in Southern New Jersey. Over the years, he got the travel bug in part from hearing his father's stories from a trip he took around the world in 1935, but also due to a desire to test his surfing skills in bigger waves.

After college, Harvey found his calling in education, and over the course of thirty-five years, he worked at various schools in Philadelphia, Oregon, and Delaware, serving as a teacher, coach, and school administrator. In addition to his work with children, his perspective on life was profoundly impacted by his Quaker upbringing and a two-year surfing trip he took around the world, which is the subject of this book.

In his retirement, he continues to work with nuclear disarmament groups, underserved children's programs, and environmental initiatives, in addition to his garden, and yet will always make time for a quick trip to the beach and the surf, if the weather is right.

www.ingramcontent.com/pod-product-compliance
Lightning Source LLC
Chambersburg PA
CBHW071224090426
42736CB00014B/2959